FINDING

IN GOD'S WORD

JOYCE L. VILLENEUVE

Printed in the United States of America
ISBN 978-1-6319201-6-5

All Scripture quotations taken from the King James Version of the Bible.

To God be the glory.

ACKNOWLEDGEMENTS

This book could not have come to fruition without the support of my husband, Martin. Thank you for encouraging me to do what God has called me to do in spite of the financial hardship that came with that calling.

To my three beautiful, wonderful children—Kathryn, John-Michael and Francesca: Each of you is my favorite child, my pride and joy, because each one of you is a special gift from God. Being your mother has been the most fulfilling role of my life. I praise God for entrusting each of you to my care. Seeing the incredible people of God that you have grown to be fills my heart with tenderness and love for you. I thank God for each of you every day and pray that you will continue to grow in your faith and love, trusting in Him always, no matter what trials or tribulations you may face in the future.

To my parents, Patricia and Govinden: Thank you for your legacy of faith and for teaching me the true meaning of family.

A HUMBLE DESIRE

I thank God for the brokenness, pain and sorrow from which this book was born. It is my humble desire that God would use my story to bring hope, strength, and courage to those who can relate to similar trials and tribulations in their life, and those who are struggling with unforgiveness.

Unforgiveness is a stronghold of the evil one who uses it to hold a person captive. I know this because I was a captive for a very long time and lost many years to depression—and a darkness so deep that I was brought to the point of suicide because of my inability to forgive.

Today, I am free because through God's Word, the Holy Bible, I found the courage to forgive. It is only my complete trust in God that has brought me to that place of grace and surrender to His will, and He has blessed and redeemed me because of my willingness to forgive and to trust Him completely. No matter how deep the pain, no matter how painful the sorrow, no matter if I understand the circumstances or not, I choose to trust in God and His mercy completely.

My humble prayer is that you, too, will find that place of grace, that place of hope, as you discover God's promises and plans for you in the Bible.

May He fill you with the Holy Spirit and flood you with an extra measure of grace and courage to face unforgiveness in your life. May He protect you and bring you to that place of complete surrender and healing. In the precious and powerful name of Jesus I pray. AMEN

CONTENTS

INTRODUCTION

"How did you do it? How did you find that deep grace to forgive all that had been done to you?"

As I looked into the interviewer's eyes, I saw the deep pain reflected in them—a pain that made him ask the question that he had been seeking an answer to for a very long time.

And I knew that my answer had the potential to change this young man's life forever.

Part 1

———⚬⚬⚬———

How Do I Forgive Myself?

The Humility of a Sinful Woman

Scripture reading: Luke 7:36-50

She came quietly to Simon's house. She had heard that Jesus had been invited to a meal with Simon. What were her plans? Had she come just to listen to the conversation going on at the table, as was typical of those times? Perhaps she thought she would be able to anoint Jesus' feet with the perfumed oil she carried in the little alabaster flask, after His feet had been washed by Simon's servants when He entered the house, as was the tradition of those times.

We don't know her name. We only know that she was a woman of ill repute. We do not know what had caused her to become a woman of ill repute either. Did she have bills to pay and no husband to help her? Was she unskilled and therefore had no opportunity to take care of herself through honest work? Had she been abused and thus propelled into a life of sin? We don't know. Only she and God knew. Yet, she came. Uninvited. But hopeful. Humble. Thankful.

Can you imagine what it took for her to show up at this Pharisee's house? Can you imagine the courage it took for her to come to the feet of Jesus? Can you imagine the scorn and disdain with which she would have been received? What could have brought her there in spite of all she knew she would face?

Yet, she came. In faith, she came, and she brought her shame, her sin, and her repentance to the one Person she knew would not look down on her and would not belittle her, but instead would have compassion on her and recognize the forgiveness that had transformed her heart. She came, bringing her tattered self-image, her battered spirit, and the woundedness in her heart. Perhaps she had heard Jesus talk about God's love and forgiveness. So, she came, because her faith told her that God had forgiven her, and she wanted to show Jesus her gratitude at being forgiven and her humble acceptance of God's love.

She came with humility. She stood silently behind Him, at His feet, weeping. As her tears fell on His feet, she began to wash His feet. The feet that should have been washed by Simon's servants. Using her tears to clean the dust and dirt off them. She did not have a basin of water—just her tears. Tears of sorrow, perhaps? Maybe tears of regret? Tears of repentance, gratitude and acceptance, definitely. How her tears must have flowed for her to have been able to wash His dirty and dusty feet!

Then she began to kiss and dry His feet with her hair. She did not bring a towel to dry His feet. Instead, she used what is a woman's crowning glory—her hair—to wipe His feet dry. Letting down her hair in public like that would have been considered shameful, but she didn't care. She wiped His feet anyway. Finally, she anointed them with the fragrant oil from her little alabaster flask. She gave the most expensive item she had—fragrant oil, probably worth a year's wages—showing her love and gratitude.

She knew she was not worthy. Yet, her faith brought her to His feet—the feet of the Person where she knew forgiveness was to be found. And what did she find? Not harsh words, or disdain, but words of compassion…forgiveness…grace…redemption. Jesus confirmed that her faith had saved her and her sins had been forgiven. Right there, in front of everyone. He looked at her with tenderness. He did not despise her—He affirmed her. Not only did He affirm her, but He redeemed her in front of the Pharisee, giving much value and worthiness to her actions.

The Bible says that Jesus told Simon in Luke 7:44-46, "*I entered into thine house, thou gavest me no water for my feet: but she hath washed my feet with tears, and wiped [them] with the hairs of her head. Thou gavest me no kiss: but this woman since the time I came in hath not ceased to kiss my feet. My head with oil thou didst not anoint: but this woman hath anointed my feet with ointment.*"

Jesus knew that she had repented for what she had done, just from the way she wept, letting her tears wash His dusty feet and wiping His feet with her hair. He saw the humility of her actions. He knew that she was sorry for the life of sin that she had been living. He knew she had faith that she had been forgiven and had humbly come to His feet with a contrite heart, seeking only to show her gratitude and her love.

Jesus did not require any great works from this woman. He knew she had already reaped the consequences of her sin, just from the way Simon, the Pharisee scorned her. Just from the way Simon shunned her leads me to believe that perhaps there were others in the town who also looked down on her. She had no worth or value in Simon's eyes, because the Scripture reveals the thoughts he had about her when he wondered how Jesus could let her touch Him.

But, Jesus gave her worth and value. All the time that she was washing His feet with her tears and drying them with her hair, He would have had His back to her and His face to Simon. However, once He had told Simon that she had treated Him better than Simon, who was supposed to be the host (and typically, in those times, he would have greeted Jesus with a kiss and would have ensured that his servants washed Jesus' feet and anointed His hair with perfumed olive oil), Jesus turned His back on Simon and looked directly at this repentant woman. In that tender look, He showed His love, He confirmed that she had been forgiven, and He affirmed her as a child of God.

Forgiveness, Grace and Redemption

The Scripture of the sinful woman is full of humility, tenderness and redemption. I love this Scripture passage because I have found myself several times at the feet of Christ, begging for forgiveness. I don't lead the kind of life that this woman is said to have lived, but I have sinned and gone against the Word of God and I have had to seek forgiveness. Most of us experience situations in life that bring us to our knees and leave us with doubts about God's love and, perhaps, even anger against Him.

One such incident that happened to me about fifteen years ago ended up being a shattered dream. I had gotten a very prestigious job, and I was doing extremely well. I had everything going for me at that particular time: a beautiful condo, cars, credit cards, long business lunches, and prestige. Everything I touched seemed to reap rewards. But it was not the right job for me, and I heard God telling me to give up the job. I typically pray about everything, and I have conversations with God about everything and anything. Sometimes, I wonder if I don't tire Him out with my incessant conversations and observations.

But, for some reason, I had not prayed about that position, or asked God if it was the right job for me. Perhaps it was because, deep down, I knew what the answer would have been. So, I battled with God over relinquishing the job. How could He give me all these skills and talents and success, and then tell me that this was not the right job for me? I looked for every excuse not to give it up.

I was raised in the Christian faith from birth and I have had a personal relationship with Jesus since I was thirteen years old. I love God and am passionate about Jesus. I have always been faithful to God and His calling on my life, so finally, in obedience to Him, I did as He asked and gave up that job. It was one of the hardest things I had ever had to do, career-wise. All the way home, all I could think of was that it was over. All the sacrifices, all the hard work, the dreams—over.

What I did not admit to myself at that time was the real reason I loved that job. You see for the very first time in my life, my parents had told me how proud they were of me when I got that position. Here I was, more than thirty years old, and I was still seeking my parents' approval! Sure, this was a high-level executive position with a lot of status, but it was the wrong job for me (as I found out much later).

I tried to make believe that everything was okay, while inside a little part of me died. I buried my feelings over the following months, trying to be strong for my family, especially my children. Instead, anger started to fester inside of me. I was angry at God and began to turn away from Him and harden my heart against Him. I didn't realize it at the time, but in doing so, I gave Satan an entry into my heart and he inflamed this anger against God. Oh boy, did he have a field day! He had me twisting so much I didn't know if I was coming or going. My life was in chaos.

The anger festered so fiercely in my heart for a few months that I finally became really sick. Irregular heartbeats, feelings of suffocation, panic attacks, and chest pains sent me on trip after trip to the doctor and the emergency room. The doctors could find nothing wrong. However, I knew I had to get my health back, so I turned to exercise. I started walking. The fresh air and exercise helped me to start thinking again and to begin to face the pain buried deep in my heart and the deep anger and disappointment I felt against God.

About eight months after walking out on what I believed was my dream job, and walking blatantly and willfully away from my faith, I came face to face with myself and with God. I don't know what it was about that particular day. Maybe it was just my heart finally getting to a place of being open to receiving what God was about to do in my life.

Tears started to flow down my cheeks, and I found myself talking to the Lord. "Why, Lord?" I remember asking. "Why did you allow me to be so successful, only to take it all away from me? I was faithful to you. In all the trials I went through, I honored you. I was a good daughter, a good sister, a good wife, and a good mother. Why would you take the only thing that I had worked so hard to achieve? Why could you not give me this one thing?"

I remember falling on my knees sobbing.

"Why?" I wailed. "Why did you abandon me?"

The Bible says in Proverbs 19:3, "*The foolishness of man perverteth his way: and his heart fretteth against the Lord.*" And that is exactly what I was doing. I had made the terrible decision to walk away blatantly and willfully from God and yet, here I was asking Him why He had left me! I was blaming God for my poor decision.

I'll never forget what happened next. All of a sudden, everything seemed to become still around me. Where a few minutes ago there had been several other joggers and walkers, now there was no one else on that walking path. The warm tropical breeze stopped blowing. Even the birds were silent. Nothing moved. I felt like I was on holy ground, in the presence of the Lord. Everything was just so quiet and silent.

Then, I heard it.

"I never left you," He whispered in the still air.

"I never left you," He whispered in the still air.

Forever engraved on my mind is an image of Christ holding me in His arms, as I laid my head against Him and wept. Each layer of pain, anguish, and hurt carried since childhood was peeled open. For the first time in a long while, I wept for me. For lost dreams and almost losing my family.

You see, God showed me that had I stayed in that job, I would have lost my husband and children. I was obsessed with that position and was already beginning to neglect my home and my family. Sure, I made sure my children had a home-cooked meal every day and that the house was clean, and the laundry done. I drove the children to school, and I went to all of their activities etc.

But once I had everything in place, I rushed back to that job, sometimes until the wee hours of the morning. I was addicted to the prestige. That job had become my idol. I wasn't spending as much time as I used to in communion with God. It was all about the job. I was becoming prideful and selfish. It was hard to swallow that truth, and I wept and prayed for God's forgiveness. I repented and like that woman at Jesus' feet, I was forgiven. God took me back.

As I accepted God's forgiveness with great humility, I also found the courage to forgive myself. Admittedly, there are times when I remember that incident and think to myself, "Gosh, how could I have done that? How could I have walked away from God? How could I have let myself get to the point of almost losing my family?" And then I feel the churnings of regret, but I stop myself and remember that God has forgiven me. As the Bible says, as far as the east is from the west, He does not hold it against me. He has forgiven all of my iniquities.

God is a God of second chances…and third chances…and fourth chances…and… however many chances are needed to bring you closer to being like Jesus. You only have to watch the news and see how people who really, really mess up are given a chance to change and to succeed. It's important to accept those second (or more chances) so that you can honor God with your life. I was given a second chance, and I went on to be successful in the calling that God called me to after I surrendered to Him.

I had the privilege of working on programs and campaigns where thousands of lives were impacted, thousands of babies saved from abortion, countless marriages strengthened, and millions of dollars raised for global mission work. I have succeeded in personal business ventures in ways that I had never imagined. But, most importantly, I now have an incredible personal relationship with Jesus Christ and a strong daily communion with God.

I don't know what you have gone through in life, the hurts and pains that have been inflicted on you, or the struggles you are facing today. I have no idea of the sufferings that hold you captive, day after day and keep you awake at night. Perhaps like me, you had a career that you thought was ideal, so, you worked hard and you were faithful and loyal to your employer for many, many years—only to be laid off—and you feel the anguish as you struggle financially, wondering how you are going to make ends meet.

I know what that's like. I've been there. I helped raise millions of dollars for a prominent ministry, only to be let go when the recession hit. I don't feel any anger or bitterness towards that ministry, as I believe being laid off was part of God's larger plan for me. I accepted it as such and have moved on to other new adventures. I was blessed in publishing a book and becoming a speaker—accomplishments I never would have achieved had I not been laid off.

By God's grace, I was able to look at that event as part of God's bigger plan for me, rather than a burden. I am able to look at my many years at that ministry as a time of preparation for this new journey that God has me on. God has allowed me to use my story of forgiveness, grace, and redemption to draw others into a closer personal relationship with His Son, Jesus Christ, and into a trusting relationship with Him.

Perhaps you had a wonderful marriage or a cherished relationship that was taken away from you, and you are angry and bitter as a result. I almost lost my husband and children because my eyes were veiled with pride and ego. I am humbled to remember that I was saved from that loss.

Perhaps you have a dream that has not come to fruition, and you keep asking God "When? When will it be my turn? When do I get to see my dream, my heart's desire come true?" And you find yourself becoming bitter as the years pass and that dream fades. Have you ever considered that maybe, just maybe, it is not God's dream and plan for you? In Jeremiah 29:11, God promises that His plans for us are plans for a future and hope, not plans of woe or evil. Do you trust that? Do you believe in God's promises?

What is holding you back from accepting God's full forgiveness? Is it pride? Ego? Anger at God for shattered dreams—dreams you had that never came to fruition? Is it a lack of faith? Or, have you even walked away from your faith like I did?

What is it?

The Bible tells us that God forgives when there is true repentance and a contrite heart asking for forgiveness. Does your faith allow you to believe this?

As humans, we tend to be hard on ourselves. We usually have compassion for other people when they fall, we rush to help them get back on their feet again, we quote Scripture that tells of God's grace and forgiveness, but heaven help us if *we* fall from grace. We beat ourselves up over and over again, even after God has forgiven us. Why do we do that? Why can we not show the same compassion to ourselves that we show to others? What is it that holds us back from fully accepting God's forgiveness? Is it a feeling of unworthiness? Do you have a misplaced anger toward God for not giving you your heart's desire? God doesn't give us everything we want—rather, He gives us everything we need, the things that are for our wellbeing, as promised in Jeremiah 29:11.

If you are struggling with unforgiveness towards yourself, pause for a moment and ask yourself this question.

By not forgiving myself, am I allowing my pride and ego to come before God's truth?

This is a tough question—one that I have struggled with several times as I've sought and received God's forgiveness. When I fell from grace and God forgave me and took me back, I continued to ask myself, "How could God forgive me?" I had failed Him. I had purposefully and willfully walked away from Him, and yet, He had taken me back and forgiven me. Even when I walked away from Him, He had continued to show me great love. I struggled to forgive myself until I came to the realization that *God, the Almighty*, had chosen to forgive me. He loved me enough to send His only Son to die for my sins so that I might have eternal life. If He was willing to forgive me, then who was I to not forgive myself? Not only does He forgive my sins, but He keeps no count of them after they have been forgiven, so why would I hold on to my sins? What good does it do me to hold on to them?

Most importantly, have I truly accepted God's forgiveness if I still hold on to unforgiveness towards myself? You cannot say that God has forgiven you, if you cannot forgive yourself. Either you truly and fully accept God's forgiveness, and let go of all the guilt and shame, or you don't.

Holding on to unforgiveness creates a barrier between you and God. It prevents and hinders you from seeing all the plans that God has for you. It stops you from receiving all the blessings that God has in store for you.

Knowing all of this, why are you still holding on to that pain of unforgiveness?

The Shame of Judas

Scripture readings: Luke 21:37-38, Luke 22:1-6, Luke 22:21-22, Luke 22:47-48

There are many thoughts and observations about Judas and his betrayal of Jesus.

Some believe he was predestined for that role, while others assert that he was specifically chosen for the role he played in Jesus' death. Yet another theory is that Judas was just plain bad. The purpose of this chapter is not to judge or defend any of the theories out there, but rather, to look at the consequences of Judas' decision to betray Jesus.

Luke 6:12-16 says, *"And it came to pass in those days, that he [Jesus] went out into a mountain to pray, and continued all night in prayer to God. And when it was day, he called [unto him] his disciples: and of them he chose twelve, whom also he named apostles; Simon, (whom he also named Peter,) and Andrew his brother, James and John, Philip and Bartholomew, Matthew and Thomas, James the [son] of Alphaeus, and Simon called Zelotes, And Judas [the brother] of James, and Judas Iscariot, which also was the traitor."*

Twelve disciples were handpicked by Jesus, after He spent an entire night in prayer to the Father. They followed Him everywhere during His earthly ministry. They walked and traveled with Him. Slept where He slept. Broke bread with Him. They learned at His feet. They prayed with Him. They witnessed the miracles. Yet, one of them would end up being a traitor and would betray Jesus up to the temple priests and guards for thirty pieces of silver.

Did Jesus know that Judas Iscariot was the disciple who would betray Him when He picked him to be one of His twelve disciples? It seems as though He did, for it says in John 6:64, *"But there are some of you that believe not. For Jesus knew from the beginning who they were that believed not, and who should betray him."* The Scriptures do not tell us how much Jesus knew when He selected Judas to be one of His apostles. The Father knew, as the Father knows and sees all, yet the Father still guided Jesus to pick Judas. It is interesting that this apostle who Jesus handpicked would be the one to betray Him. Not one of the Pharisees who hated Jesus so much. Not a member of the Sanhedrin. Not one of the scribes. But one of Jesus' chosen few—a member from His inner sanctum of chosen apostles: Judas Iscariot.

Why did Judas betray Jesus? What was his motive in doing so? Was he jealous of Jesus' relationship with some of the other apostles? Did he perceive himself to be somehow lower than the other disciples, since he came from a different area than the others? Had Jesus reprimanded him, whereupon his anger against Jesus festered until he found a way to get even? Was he a political zealot? Or was it truly the greed and love of money that drove him to betray the Master?

First Timothy 6:10 says, *"For the love of money is the root of all evil: which while some coveted after, they have erred from the faith, and pierced themselves through with many sorrows."*

It seems from Scripture that Judas had a particular weakness for money. In fact, in John 12:6, it says, *"This he said, not that he cared for the poor; but because he was a thief, and had the bag, and bare what was put therein."* In other words, Judas would help himself to the money that he was entrusted with. This weakness for money is what allowed Satan to tempt Judas, as is described in Luke 22:3, *"Then entered Satan into Judas surnamed Iscariot, being of the number of the twelve."*

From that moment, Judas began to negotiate with the high priests and temple guards about how he would deliver Jesus over to them, and for what price. He knew that Jesus spent His evenings on the Mount of Olives, so it would be relatively easy to find a time to hand Jesus over to them. Did he haggle over the price? Or, was it easy to get the price he wanted, since the high priests were already trying to figure out how to get Jesus?

Thirty pieces of silver...what an awful price tag for anyone's life, let alone the Savior's!

In Matthew 26:24, Jesus said, "*The Son of man goeth as it is written of him: but woe unto that man by whom the Son of man is betrayed! it had been good for that man if he had not been born.*" By saying this, Jesus let all of His disciples know that He knew He was about to be betrayed by one of them, and He warned what would happen to the person who betrayed Him. Was He giving the potential traitor a chance to change his mind, perhaps? But Judas did not change his mind. He continued as planned. He entered the Mount of Olives, surrounded by many guards with weapons. He went to Jesus, leaned in, and then he betrayed Jesus with the most intimate of gestures—a kiss—a gesture usually reserved for those we love and care about. A gesture that led Jesus to ask, as the Bible records in Luke 22:48, "*... Judas, betrayest thou the Son of Man with a kiss?*"

Filled with remorse after his betrayal of Jesus, Judas tried to give the money back to the chief priest and elders. He tried to make amends for what he had done. He tried to absolve his guilt. They refused to take the money back, so Judas threw it down on the temple floor and left. Matthew 27:3-10, makes it clear that Judas repented and was filled with remorse for what he had done. But he was unable to forgive himself. Filled with despair and without hope, he hanged himself.

Like all of us, Judas had the free will to choose between right and wrong. He chose wrong because he had allowed his weakness and love of money to give Satan a stronghold in his life. Even though Judas repented and was remorseful about what he had done, he was blinded by Satan and could not see God's goodness. He had walked with Jesus, heard His teachings, eaten the same bread as Jesus, and yet did not fully understand that Jesus had come to save us from sin, that He was about to give His life's blood to obtain our very salvation. He was blinded to the love of Jesus by his love and greed of money. If only Judas had gone to the Father when he had repented and been remorseful. If only he had asked for God's forgiveness, how different the rest of his life could have been! If only he had believed in the saving grace of Jesus!

But that is what Satan does. He blinds us to God's goodness. He uses our shame to stop us from having a relationship of true intimacy with God. He uses our shame and sin to hold us captive and prevents us from seeing that if we repent and come to God with a contrite heart, God can and will change our hearts and forgive us. Satan holds our shame and uses it to lure us into more sin—building a wall of one sin after another until we feel hopeless, lost, and completely undeserving of forgiveness.

But, this is not true!

God has given us the free will to choose to come to Him, turn away from our sin, and ask for forgiveness. He yearns for that deep relationship with us, and loves us enough to not force us to do anything against our will. We have to come to Him in humility and willingly surrender our evil ways. We have to repent and ask for His grace and mercy.

And we have to believe that Jesus Christ, His Son, is our Lord and Savior and that Jesus died for our sins. We have to work hard to not sin again. How often do we read in the Bible where Jesus forgave someone and said, "Go and sin no more?" That's what true repentance is about: turning away from the sin, and then trying our best to not repeat it. God knows we are human. He knows we will fall short many times. But He willingly forgives us when we repent. He forgives us time and time again.

Have you ever done something that has separated you from your relationship with God? Are you overwhelmed by guilt and cannot see a way out? Do you feel the remorse of your actions? Then take heart! God is simply waiting for you to ask for His forgiveness. Repent of whatever it is that is holding you captive and break that chain that Satan has you tangled in. Rip that veil of shame or hopelessness away from your eyes and surrender to God's will, asking Him to forgive you. Believe in the redeeming power of Jesus' death on the cross for your sins.

Never, Ever, Lose Hope.

Second Corinthians 4:8-10 says, *"[We are] troubled on every side, yet not distressed; [we are] perplexed, but not in despair; Persecuted, but not forsaken; cast down, but not destroyed; Always bearing about in the body the dying of the Lord Jesus, that the life also of Jesus might be made manifest in our body."* When we find ourselves in that dark place, where despair takes over the mind, we need to remember why Jesus died. We need to remember His suffering. We need to remember the ransom He paid for us. We need to remember that He has paid all of our debts, all of our sins have been forgiven, and our redemption has been secured. Most of all, we need to remember God's unconditional love.

> God is simply waiting for you to ask for His forgiveness.

Do not allow yourself to get into the pit of hell—that place where there seems to be no solution—because that is the place where Satan wants to keep you, that place of captivity where he can steal your joy, your hope, and your happiness. Do not allow Satan to manipulate you by reminding you of the mistakes you have made.

Do not allow him to cloud your judgment and knowledge of God's goodness toward you. Instead, trust in God's unconditional love, mercy, and forgiving grace.

3

The Repentance of Peter

Scripture reading: Luke 22:54-62

I don't believe that anyone can deny Peter's love for Jesus. He had traveled for three years with Jesus and heard Jesus preach. He had seen the miracles firsthand. He had walked where Jesus walked and eaten where Jesus ate. He had learned at the Master's feet, just like Judas. He was protective of Jesus, as shown in Luke 22:50, which says, *"And one of them smote the servant of the high priest, and cut off his right ear."*

While the other apostles were scared and ran for their lives when they saw the guards coming to the Garden of Gethsemane to arrest Jesus, it was Peter who took a stand, tried to defend Jesus and cut off the ear of the servant of the high priest.

At the Last Supper, as Luke 22:31-32 says, Jesus said to Peter, *"...Simon, Simon, behold, Satan hath desired [to have] you, that he may sift [you] as wheat: But I have prayed for thee, that thy faith fail not: and when thou art converted, strengthen thy brethren."*

Peter was bold and courageous in his reply to Jesus, as recorded in Luke 22:33, *"And he said unto him, Lord, I am ready to go with thee, both into prison, and to death."* Yes, at that point, Peter was prepared to die with Jesus.

After Jesus was arrested, Peter followed at a distance to see what they were going to do to Jesus. However, when the time came and he was tested, he denied Jesus three times, just as Jesus had foretold. Luke 22:61-62 says, *"And the Lord turned, and looked upon Peter. And Peter remembered the word of the Lord, how he had said unto him, Before the cock crow, thou shalt deny me thrice. And Peter went out, and wept bitterly."*

Had Peter seen the sorrow in Jesus' eyes after Peter denied Jesus for the third time? Had he seen disappointment reflected in Jesus' body language as He was led away? Or, was that love shimmering in the Savior's eyes as He looked at Peter? Did Peter feel ashamed for denying Jesus after he had stated so boldly that he was prepared to go to prison and even suffer death with Jesus? What had caused Peter to deny Jesus?

Fear.

Peter had followed Jesus at a distance because he wanted to be with Jesus, he had been courageous in sitting outside with the temple guards in the courtyard, waiting to see what they were going to do to Jesus, but he was also fearful of being recognized as one of Jesus' followers and disciples, as that could very well have meant being arrested himself and possibly being put to death. Fear took over, leading Peter to deny Jesus. Like Judas, Peter also betrayed Jesus by denying his friendship, but his story had a different outcome. Peter wept bitterly. His heart was grieved within him. Guilt ate away at him. Shame overwhelmed him. He was remorseful and repentant just like Judas. But, the big difference between the two men was that Peter remembered why Jesus had come and who Jesus was—the Son of God. Peter did not lose hope. He was able to seek forgiveness and he was able to receive and accept forgiveness for his failing.

Peter's humility in seeking forgiveness brings him back to the very foundations of his journey with Jesus—his faith. The Bible says in Matthew 16:13-18, "*When Jesus came into the coasts of Caesarea Philippi, he asked his disciples, saying, Whom do men say that I the Son of man am? And they said, Some [say that thou art] John the Baptist: some, Elias; and others, Jeremias, or one of the prophets. He saith unto them, But whom say ye that I am? And Simon Peter answered and said, Thou art the Christ, the Son of the living God. And Jesus answered and said unto him, Blessed art thou, Simon Barjona: for flesh and blood hath not revealed [it] unto thee, but my Father which is in heaven. And I say also unto thee, That thou art Peter, and upon this rock I will build my church; and the gates of hell shall not prevail against it.*"

Peter believed that Jesus was the Son of God. He believed in Jesus' redeeming grace because the Father had revealed that to Peter, as seen in his response to Jesus, when he acknowledged that Jesus is the Son of God. With Peter's repentance came his redemption, just as Jesus had promised him. A soul was saved.

We see God's redeeming grace explained in 1 Peter 5:10, which states, "*But the God of all grace, who hath called us unto his eternal glory by Christ Jesus, after that ye have suffered a while, make you perfect, establish, strengthen, settle [you].*"

Repentance brings forgiveness. Forgiveness brings redemption. From my own journey, I can testify that every moment of failure caused by sin that I have ever experienced has brought forgiveness when I have sought it. And every moment of forgiveness has brought God's redeeming grace. He has used every single bit of my

> Repentance brings forgiveness. Forgiveness brings redemption.

pain, every tear, and every bit of sorrow to help strengthen others. Nothing has been wasted. I have suffered the consequences of my sins and bad decisions, but they have made me stronger and deepened my faith.

In Psalm 46:1-3, it says, *"God [is] our refuge and strength, a very present help in trouble. Therefore will not we fear, though the earth be removed, and though the mountains be carried into the midst of the sea; [Though] the waters thereof roar [and] be troubled, [though] the mountains shake with the swelling thereof."*

Earthquakes. Avalanches. Tsunamis. Sin. Betrayal. Afflictions. No evil that is inflicted upon us should take away our faith that God will take us to a place of safety and refuge—a place of strength, courage, and perseverance. That was the foundation that Peter stood upon—his faith. Jesus told Peter that he was about to be sifted like wheat, but He also assured Peter that He was praying that Peter's faith would see him through. And it did.

Is fear holding you back from seeking God's forgiveness? Let your faith be bigger and stronger than your fear. When fear grips you, remember the foundations of your faith! The Bible says in 2 Timothy 1:7, *"For God hath not given us the spirit of fear; but of power, and of love, and of a sound mind."* That's where we need to go when we have those terrible traumas inflicted upon us—to our foundation of faith. That's where we need to go when we fall from grace: to remember that God is our refuge and strength...to be convinced at a soul level that no matter what hardship comes our way, no matter how difficult a situation we find ourselves in, no matter what heinous sins we may commit and how badly we may fall from grace, no matter what others may do to us, God will be our refuge and our strength, and He will come to our aid. He will save us, even from ourselves and in spite of ourselves. But, we have to seek Him.

We have to seek His forgiveness. We have to repent and change. Most of all, we have to stay strong. Although we may weep, we must ensure that our foundational trust and faith in God is beyond the reach of Satan's destructive manipulations.

Part 2

How Can I Forgive Others?

The Perseverance of Job

Scripture reading: The Book of Job

We learn about the character of Job in Job 1:1, which says, *"There was a man in the land of Uz, whose name [was] Job; and that man was perfect and upright, and one that feared God, and eschewed evil."*

Job was a good man. A righteous man. A man who feared God and shunned evil—which made him a target for Satan. Satan does not like anyone who shuns or despises evil.

The Bible continues to tell us in Job 1:6-12, about a conversation between God and Satan wherein they discussed Job. During the conversation, Satan basically told God that Job was faithful to God only because God had put a hedge of protection around Job, but if Job were to lose what God had blessed him with, then surely, Job would curse God.

So, God gave Satan permission to test Job, but not to touch his person. And, Satan had a field day wreaking havoc and mayhem on Job. He lost his material possessions. His servants were killed. His sons and daughters were killed. Wracked with grief, Job tore his garments and shaved his head. But, instead of cursing God for these great losses, Job continued to praise God, saying in Job 1:21, *"... Naked came I out of my mother's womb, and naked shall I return thither: the Lord gave, and the Lord hath taken away; blessed be the name of the Lord."* He acknowledged that everything he had been blessed with, he had received at God's hands and therefore, God had the right to take it all away, if He chose to.

Seeing this, Satan told God that if Job's body were touched, he would surely curse God. God gave Satan permission again, this time to touch Job's body but not take his life. Satan struck Job with painful boils from the top of his head to the soles of his feet. Still, Job, in spite of the suffering, maintained his integrity and did not curse God.

Even when his wife told him to curse God and die, Job would not do so, replying instead as recorded in Job 2:10, "... *Thou speakest as one of the foolish women speaketh. What? shall we receive good at the hand of God, and shall we not receive evil? In all this did not Job sin with his lips.*"

Even when Job's friends came to supposedly comfort him and instead began to debate that perhaps his suffering was caused by his sin, Job still did not curse God for he knew that he had not sinned against God.

Job persevered in all of his trials and sufferings. When God finally spoke to Job and showed him all of His majestic creations and power, Job acknowledged that God is indeed sovereign. God blessed Job with double of all that he had lost during Satan's testing.

> We don't always know why God allows us to go through the trials and tribulations that we have in life.

We don't always know why God allows us to go through the trials and tribulations that we have in life. Like Job, we may be loyal and faithful to God and yet still go through difficult times. It is easy to keep the faith when everything is going well, but how do we react when things go wrong and we find ourselves in the land of suffering? Do we continue to trust God as Job did, knowing that in His timing, all will be made well? Or, do we fall away from the faith, believing that God has betrayed us?

Faith During Trials

The last seven years have been particularly difficult years for me with the passing of several close family members, especially my mother. I was laid off from a job that I believed at the time was my calling. I lost a pet whose passing left me grieving as I have never grieved the loss of a pet before. But none of that prepared me for the additional trials that I experienced this past year. While my suffering was nothing compared to Job's, my pain during this time of testing was still deep. I lost the funds that I had set aside for retirement at the hands of a family member to whom I would have entrusted my life. My once beautiful "retirement home" was in disrepair and in need of thousands of dollars of renovations, and the inheritance I had planned to leave my children some day was gone. Court cases, strife, chaos, and mayhem gripped me on a daily basis for months. My health was jeopardized. My marriage was tested. My life was ripped apart in ways that I had never expected.

So, I went to the only place I could go to—the foot of the cross.

I went to the only person I knew I could trust—God.

For months, I knelt at the foot of the cross, weeping and praying. Weeping, not so much for what I had lost, as I would have given this man everything if he had asked me for it. I wept for the inheritance that my children would not get to enjoy—the fruits of my labor and love. Every parent dreams of leaving something for their children. I wept for my marriage. Most of all, I wept because of the pain of the betrayal I felt at the hands of this much-loved family member. I prayed constantly that God would bless him, that God would not hold him accountable for what he had done to me, and that God would forgive him and fill me with the Holy Spirit and the grace to also forgive him. There were days when I didn't even have the words to pray because there just were no words. I just knelt quietly in front of that crucifix.

Not once during this time of suffering did I ask God, "Why?" because like Job, I knew that God had blessed me with so much and if He chose to take it away, then so be it. I am still alive, and as long as there is breath in me, I will continue to bless His name. God has already brought me through so much in life: war, loneliness, depression, despair, and from the brink of suicide. I knew that He would get me through this, too. Yet a part of me was concerned with all the issues and suffering that just would not end.

Then, in November 2013, as I was once again kneeling quietly in front of the crucifix, alone in a little church, I whispered the words, "Father, I am tired. I am being sifted like wheat and I am just so tired." The months of constant battling was taking its toll. I was praying for strength and courage. I desperately needed God's reassurance.

Then, I heard a whisper.

"Do you trust me?"

From somewhere deep inside of me, that place of deep sincerity and utmost faith, I responded without a nanosecond of hesitation, "Though You slay me, Lord, still will I love You, still will I trust You, still will I praise You." I meant every single word.

I was immediately filled with immense peace, and I knew that God would get me through all of this hardship. He would fight these battles for me. I just had to trust Him. I just had to keep the faith. I would still need to go through all of these trials, but I just had to persevere, like Job. In God's timing, this season of suffering will be changed into a season of joy.

That afternoon, when I got back home, I received a message from a friend who I had not seen or spoken to in years. He had found himself praying for me out of the blue, and the message that he had received was Jeremiah 29:11-14. I smiled to myself as Jeremiah 29:11-13 is my life verse, the verse I pray and hold on to and had literally clung to on a daily basis during this time of crisis. But, Jeremiah 29:14 was the interesting part for it says, *"And I will be found of you, saith the Lord: and I will turn away your captivity, and I will gather you from all the nations, and from all the places whither I have driven you, saith the Lord; and I will bring you again into the place whence I caused you to be carried away captive."*

In this, I saw God's promise to restore what has been lost. My journey of trials and tribulations are not over yet. However, I have learned to trust God. I have found patience and contentment in my suffering. I have felt, and continue to feel, God's great love for me. He has promised me that He knows the plans that He has for me, and so my faith allows me to take each day as it comes, trusting always that God is there with me. The weeping has stopped. My heart is at peace, even as I continue in the trials. I have given over my life and future into God's hands. What better place to put them?

Like Job, I continue to persevere. I continue to thank and praise God daily for all that I have and all that He has blessed me with, even the things that I have lost and the sorrow and brokenness that I have experienced, am experiencing, and will experience in the future. At the end of the day, God is sovereign. I will not ask, "Why?" but I will persevere in faith and hope, secure in the knowledge that God is indeed my refuge and strength.

Are you struggling right now? Do you feel lost in the sea of adversity? Do you feel like God has forgotten you because of all the trials and tribulations that you are going through? Do you doubt God's sovereignty? Has someone hurt you so badly that you ask how God could have allowed such tragedy into your life? Are you afraid that if you forgive someone, you will look weak?

There is great strength in forgiving someone who has hurt you. Forgiveness is not for the weak. Do you think that the person you forgive will want to resume a relationship with you, and so you do not forgive because you do not want to have a relationship with that person? You do not need to have a relationship with someone who has hurt you or traumatized you. You can forgive in your heart, just quietly between you and God.

James 1:2-5 says, *"My brethren, count it all joy when ye fall into diverse temptations; Knowing [this], that the trying of your faith worketh patience. But let patience have [her] perfect work, that ye may be perfect and entire, wanting nothing. If any of you lack wisdom, let him ask of God, that giveth to all [men] liberally, and upbraideth not; and it shall be given him."*

Keep your eyes on God like Job did. When you go through trials and hardship, don't ask the "why," but rather, ask God to give you what you need to persevere. Ask God to be your strength. Ask God to give you the courage to forgive, if that is what is needed. Ask God to give you the heart to praise Him for all that you have, all the blessings that you have ever received and not to complain about what you have lost or what you do not have. Ask God to help you to remember His sovereignty in times of trials so that you may not fall away from the faith, when things go wrong.

Most of all, trust God. Keep persevering in doing good and forgiving others even when they fail you, hurt you, and betray you. Keep praying for God to forgive them and bless them. Keep believing that the God who you love when He blesses you with plenty on the mountaintop is the same God who loves and carries you through the valley of trials and tribulations. Persevere in your trials, as James 1:12 says, *"Blessed [is] the man that endureth temptation: for when he is tried, he shall receive the crown of life, which the Lord hath promised to them that love him."*

At the end of the day, your perseverance, patience, ability to forgive and receive forgiveness, faith, and trust in God are the greatest weapons against the snares of the devil—and these will lead you right into the fullness of God's blessings.

The Faith of Abraham

Scripture readings: Genesis 12:1 to 22:23

Abraham is most known in the Bible for his faith. At seventy-five years old, he packed all of his possessions and left for lands unknown with his aging wife, Sarah. He had heard God telling him to leave his country, his family, and his father's home, and to go to a land that God would show him—a place where God would use Abraham to create a great nation. Abraham went—without questions.

As we read through all the chapters of Genesis 12 to the end of Genesis 22, we learn a lot about Abraham's character and his personal relationship with God. He heard God's voice many times. He didn't always do what was right in God's eyes, as we can see when he and Sarah went to Egypt because of the famine and Abraham allowed Sarah to be taken captive. Abraham feared for his life and told Sarah to say that she was his sister instead of his wife. But, God protected Sarah and sent plagues to Pharaoh and his house, until Pharaoh gave Sarah back to Abraham and sent them on their way.

Then, there was the promise of a son—the heir to Abraham—who was to be born of Sarah. Sarah was already past childbearing age, so it took a lot of faith to believe that God would indeed give Abraham the desire of his heart for a son. Yet, Abraham believed. For twenty five years, he believed. He hoped. And finally, he received his promised heir from God—Isaac.

The Bible says in Genesis 22:1-3, *"And it came to pass after these things, that God tested Abraham, and said unto him, Abraham: and he said, Behold, [here] I [am].* And he said, Take now thy son, thine only [son] Isaac, whom thou lovest, and get thee into the land of Moriah; and offer him there for a burnt offering upon one of the mountains which I will tell thee of. And Abraham rose up early in the morning, and saddled his ass, and took two of his young men with him, and Isaac his son, and clave the wood for the burnt offering, and rose up, and went unto the place of which God had told him."*

As a young child, I often wondered what kind of God would ask Abraham to do the unthinkable—sacrifice his only son. As I got older and understood God's own sacrifice of His only beloved Son, Jesus, for our salvation, I understood that God would not ask anything of us that He, Himself, would not do. Abraham's faith and close communion with God allowed him to know this and to do as God had asked him. Abraham did not question God. He saddled up what he would need in order to obey God and started the journey to Moriah.

Was his heart heavy within him? Was he silently grieving as he laid the wood upon Isaac's back and they began to walk to the place of offering? Or, did his words in Genesis 22: 5, which says, *"And Abraham said unto his young men, Abide ye here with the ass; and I and the lad will go yonder and worship, and come again to you"* convey total trust and confidence in God as Abraham stated that both he and Isaac would go and worship and then return. Even when Isaac asked him where the lamb for the offering was, Abraham's response was that God would provide the lamb for the burnt offering. What total trust and faith in God!

Reaching the place that God had told him, Abraham continued to build the altar. He placed the wood as needed and then tied Isaac and placed him on the altar. Then, he took the knife and raised it, ready to sacrifice his son. His only son. The heir that he had yearned for and waited twenty five years for. His son, born to him by Sarah. The son that God himself had promised to Abraham. The son of his hopes and dreams—the one who would bring forth his descendants, as promised by God. Abraham's love for God, his fear of God and his faith in God allowed him to not withhold anything from God. He fully intended to sacrifice Isaac, while hoping at the same time that somehow, God would intervene.

God saw Abraham's willingness to sacrifice his son to Him and God supplied a ram in the thicket that Abraham sacrificed instead. After testing Abraham, God blessed Abraham with everything that He had promised to him. God will sometimes test us too—to refine our character, as he did with Abraham. He will test us so that our Christ-like character may be a beacon to others—to show that Satan's attacks cannot blemish our faith, just as Satan tried with Job.

By continuing to show faith in God during times of struggle and times of adversity, even when He asks for our "Isaacs"—that which we love the most—we show that we can truly trust God, and we can lead others who are watching us during those times to find faith in God, if they too are going through a season of pain and struggles.

God will sometimes test us too—to refine our character...

But, God will never tempt us. In James 1:13-14, the Bible says, *"Let no man say when he is tempted, I am tempted of God: for God cannot be tempted with evil, neither tempteth he any man: But every man is tempted, when he is drawn away of his own lust, and enticed."* Temptation is from Satan. When we are tempted to hurt those who have hurt us—that is of Satan. When we return evil for evil—that is of Satan. When we hold on to unforgiveness and end up being angry at God, bitter and filled with the lies of Satan, that is not of God. That is Satan creating a stronghold in us so that he can take away the joy that God has planned for us.

Satan uses trials and tribulations to manipulate and drive us away from God. He puts doubts in our minds and makes us question God's goodness. He causes discouragement and defeat to rob us of all the blessings that God has in store for us. He makes things like addictions to pornography, alcohol, drugs, irresponsible sex, the hunger for money, and prestige seem good, to divert us from God's real plans for us. God tests us to drive us towards Him, to strengthen us and to give us a life of blessing, to purify us, refine us and mold us into the image of His Son. God uses our trials and sorrows to bring glory to Him, to teach others through our testimony of faith of His steadfast love for each of us, and to teach us perseverance, patience and contentment in all things.

Abraham's faith allowed him to surrender everything to God—his whole future and the promise of his descendants through Isaac. In Genesis 22:15-18, it says, *"And the angel of the Lord called unto Abraham out of heaven the second time, And said, By myself have I sworn, saith the Lord, for because thou hast done this thing, and hast not withheld thy son, thine only [son]: That in blessing I will bless thee, and in multiplying I will multiply thy seed as the stars of the heaven, and as the sand which [is] upon the sea shore; and thy seed shall possess the gate of his enemies; And in thy seed shall all the nations of the earth be blessed; because thou hast obeyed my voice."* God blessed Abraham for his faith and trust.

When we follow God's mandate to forgive others or to seek His forgiveness when we fall from grace, God blesses us. He blesses our faith, much as He did for Abraham. He blesses our trust, just as He did for Job. He restores peace and contentment in our hearts, and He fulfills His plans for our future because those are His promises to us. Faith allows us to forgive what we think is unforgivable because faith sends us to the foot of the cross where grace and mercy abounds.

The Trust of Joseph

Scripture reading: Genesis 37:1 to 50:1-26

One of the most difficult challenges in the journey of forgiveness is forgiving broken relationships. This is perhaps the topic that affects most people because life is about relationships. It is the area that most people find themselves broken over. Whether it is a broken relationship with a parent, an unresolved issue with a sibling, a crisis situation with a co-worker, a painful encounter with a stranger, or unresolved issues with children, this is the area that most people anguish over.

I have heard many things as I travel and speak at conferences and retreats. Things like, "How do I forgive my brother for taking my life's savings?" Or, "My mother abused me for so many years. She was supposed to love and protect me. How could she do that?" Or, "My Dad and I haven't spoken in thirty years." Or, "My sister hasn't spoken to me for a long time and I don't know what I have done to offend her. She just ignores me" Or, "My co-worker humiliates me in front of the team. I don't know why." And the heartbreaking one, "I was brutally raped by a stranger. How do I forgive that person and go on?"

How do we find that deeper grace to forgive those situations that in our minds are unforgivable?

These situations can hold us captive and can prevent us from moving on in the abundant life that God desires for us, if we hold on to unforgiveness. Yet, how can we move past them? How do we find that deeper grace to forgive those situations that in our minds are unforgivable?

One of the examples that we can turn to in the Bible on broken relationships is the story of Joseph. In Genesis 37:1 to Genesis 50:1-26, we learn about Joseph, the favorite son of Jacob. Jacob favored Joseph because Joseph was born to him in Jacob's old age. He gave Joseph a beautiful coat which made his other sons jealous of Joseph. As a parent, it is never wise to show favoritism between your children. However, Joseph also fueled his brothers' jealousy by telling them about the prophetic dreams that he was having; a vision that God had given Joseph of what his life would be like as he got older, and dreams that showed his brothers bowing down to Joseph.

So, when the opportunity arose to get rid of Joseph, the brothers did. They sold him into slavery, and he ended up in Egypt and imprisoned for many years. However, what the brothers had meant for evil, God meant for good. Through a series of events, God raised Joseph to become one of the most influential men in Egypt, next to the pharaoh. Joseph had a lot of power, and he could have used that power for revenge against his brothers, when they found themselves before him seeking food during the famine. But Joseph had a very different reaction from what we would expect. Most people would feel angry, even bitter or vengeful, at such a betrayal. But not Joseph.

In Genesis 45:1-8, the Bible says, "*Then Joseph could not refrain himself before all them that stood by him; and he cried, "Cause every man to go out from me!" And there stood no man with him, while Joseph made himself known unto his brethren. And he wept aloud: and the Egyptians and the house of Pharaoh heard. And Joseph said unto his brethren, I am Joseph; doth my father yet live? And his brethren could not answer him; for they were troubled at his presence. And Joseph said unto his brethren, Come near to me, I pray you. And they came near. And he said, I am Joseph your brother, whom ye sold into*

Egypt. Now therefore be not grieved, nor angry with yourselves, that ye sold me hither: for God did send me before you to preserve life. For these two years hath the famine been in the land: and yet there are five years, in which there shall neither be plowing nor harvest. And God sent me before you to preserve you a posterity in the earth, and to save your lives by a great deliverance. So now it was not you that sent me hither, but God: and he hath made me a father to Pharaoh, and lord of all his house, and a ruler throughout all the land of Egypt."

Joseph wept when he saw his brothers. He wept so loudly that the Egyptians and the house of Pharaoh heard him. Was he weeping from the ache that must have been in his heart for years from being betrayed and sold into slavery by the very brothers he thought loved him? Maybe. Did he weep because he realized that the visions he had as a youth were about to come to fruition. Perhaps. Could he have been weeping from the joy of seeing his brothers? He sent his court out so that they would not witness what he was about to say to his brothers. *He hid their shame.* He wept because his heart was filled with grace, joy, and a mixture of grief and love. He asked about his father. And then, he gave them the biggest gift that one can give to a person who has offended or betrayed you: forgiveness. He reassured his brothers that God had planned this and had sent him ahead so that he could be in a place and position to save them and their families from the famine. God had delivered them.

Joseph had trusted God. He had believed in the visions that God had given him, and although God tested Joseph and he went through many trials and tribulations, he suffered them faithfully, believing that in the right timing, God would deliver him from all the hardships he was enduring. And God did. By raising Joseph to a place of high esteem, God enabled Joseph to be ready to forgive his brothers and to save them from famine. God had seen into the future and had allowed Joseph to be sold into slavery because He had already planned how He was going to use that evil to save the lives of

Joseph's brothers. During his time of trial and captivity, Joseph learnt humility, patience, perseverance, trust and forgiveness.

Many times when we have been hurt, we plan revenge on the person who has offended us or we wish harm on them—punishment, if you will. It is interesting to note that Joseph did not feel anger or animosity towards his brothers when they faced him. I believe that over the years God had worked on Joseph's heart, and he had come to a place of grace and deep understanding, believing that God had allowed him to go through all he had for a reason. His trials would result in saving his family from famine and delivering them into safety in Egypt. That was part of God's bigger plan.

Joseph was given a vision, but he endured slavery and prison before seeing it come to fruition more than a decade later. Our answers from God do not always come in the weeks and months when we desire them. They may take years: Years of perseverance. Years of trusting God. Years of believing in Him. But His promises will *always* come to fruition. Are you crying out to God today? Be encouraged. His answer will come in due time. We don't always know why God allows hardships and trials in our lives, but those moments refine us. They bring us closer to God if we allow them, and most of all, they are moments of testing that can be used to glorify Him. Trusting God, even when we do not understand why we are going through the difficult circumstances that we find ourselves in, allows God to redeem us and use us for His glory.

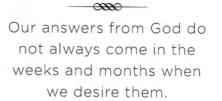

Our answers from God do not always come in the weeks and months when we desire them.

Answering the Call

I have gone through many trials that have led me to a place of deep trust in God. I do not offer these testimonies for any personal glory, or to bring shame or anguish to anyone involved, but to show God's redeeming love.

I was born and raised in Uganda until I was about twelve, when Idi Amin took over the country. The coup was bloody, and during his reign of terror, thousands of people were killed or disappeared—never to be heard from again. I saw things during that time that I hope and pray my children and their children never have to see. I still get nightmares from seeing five men brutally beaten and then burned alive. I still remember hearing their screams and smelling their burning hair and flesh. That horrible experience scarred me.

It's hard to explain the trauma of seeing people die in front of you or describe the fear of bullets flying over your home during the coup, or bombs bursting in the air day after day, and not knowing whether you were going to survive. It does something to your psyche. More than forty years ago, you didn't hear much about Post-Traumatic Stress Disorder. I don't even know if doctors knew how to treat it at that time. I have no doubt that I left Uganda with PTSD.

And years later, all of that fear and trauma surfaced after an awful experience in a prominent Christian ministry. But first, some context…

For many years while I was growing up, I dreamed of becoming a nun. I wanted to dedicate my life to serving God and His people, and I believed the only way to do that was by becoming a nun. At the age of twenty-three, after my second attempt to join a convent two years earlier had failed, I had the privilege of meeting Mother Teresa from Calcutta. She was what I wanted to be—a bearer of God's love to the poor, His hands and feet to those in need. After I expressed my disappointment to Mother Teresa about not being accepted into the convent, she looked at me and said gently, "You do not need to wear a nun's garment to do God's work. Continue to pray, and He will give you the desire of your heart when it is time."

I remembered those words the first day I started working at a prominent Christian ministry shortly after our family moved from Guam to the United States. After a series of interviews, I accepted a one-week tryout as an account coordinator in the creative department at the ministry. The manager was intrigued by why someone with so much experience and high-level marketing background would insist on coming on board at the lowest level possible. But I had to find myself again after my crazy walk away from the church and back again, and I didn't want to jeopardize my relationship with God by jumping into a management position. I wanted to start at the bottom and work back up, according to God's will.

By Thursday of my first week at the ministry, I knew I was exactly where I was meant to be. On Friday morning a headhunter called to offer me an executive position at a five-star resort. I said with a smile in my voice, "No thanks. I have found the job that is my calling, if they will have me."

"Well, we'll offer you more money. How much do you want?"

"You've already offered me four times what this job pays," I replied, laughing out loud. "But it is not about the money. It is about a calling, and this is what I have wanted to do all my life. I just hope they will have me."

A few minutes after I hung up with the headhunter, the ministry offered me the job. The manager still did not understand my desire to start at such a low level, but I just smiled, knowing this was going to be an incredible journey. During my years at the ministry, I worked on campaigns and programs that had a huge global impact, which humbled me daily. My heart had desired this for so long. I was fulfilling a clear mission with the talents God had given me. The ministry was strong and wonderful: Being a part of it restored my soul in many ways.

About four years into my work there, however, I faced a situation that threatened to crush me again. April 8, 2003, started like any other day. At work, I had just received new artwork for a project I was overseeing, so it was an exciting day. Just before a late-afternoon meeting, I stopped by a co-worker's office to share my excitement about the artwork. As we were chatting, a male coworker came up to me and made a general comment. Then he suddenly hit me several times on the left arm. I was taken aback and stepped away from the office, only to have him slap me a few more times, but on my right arm. I took a step backward from him and turned away, at which point he hit me between my shoulder blades. I spun around and held up my hands in front of me—a clear indication to stop. Fortunately, he stopped. I was shocked. I had no idea what had just happened. I know some men fool around with other men, hitting and shoving each other like football players do, but I had never participated in anything like that, nor had I given this man any reason to believe that what he had just done was acceptable behavior. That evening, as I took off my suit jacket, my husband gasped.

"What happened to your arm?" he said.

"Oh, a male coworker hit me today," I answered, turning my head to look at my left arm. I was shocked to see welts on it. My right arm also had red marks on it, as did my back.

"What?" yelled my husband. He was beside himself and wanted to go to the ministry the next day to confront the man who had hit me. That is where I made my first mistake. I told him no, as I wanted to protect the image of the ministry. I could imagine the press getting a hold of this situation and blowing it out of proportion.

"I will handle the situation with this man tomorrow, the way we are supposed to in a Christian environment," I said, intending to confront my coworker first alone. That was my second mistake. I should have realized that this situation could be explosive and should have been handled by Human Resources personnel right from the beginning. Instead, I confronted the male coworker the next day. While he apologized and indicated he intended no malice, the situation was too difficult for either one of us to deal with. A week later, it all came to a head when he stood outside my office and asked if I was okay.

"No, I'm not," I replied. "I'm struggling with what happened."

I was upset; I could not sleep or eat properly. I kept reliving the moment when I was physically struck. I didn't know it at the time, but I was beginning to show the signs of PTSD.

"I can't believe I could have done what you said I did," he said. He walked into my office and sat down.

"You hit me!" I hissed between clenched teeth. "I have a witness who can tell you exactly what you did!"

"Well, let me talk to this witness then. I could never do anything like this!" He was struggling, too.

Agreeing to meet with him and the other co-worker without any Human Resources personnel in a conference room was my third mistake. He was livid when the witness repeated what she had seen: He realized that his actions had been violent and had been witnessed by someone else. He started accusing me of having an "agenda" and said that my husband probably abused me and now I was blaming him. That's when I knew the situation was way out of hand. I was afraid he would strike me again, so I quietly got up and headed out the door. He was yelling as I left, but I went straight to my office.

A whirlwind of meetings with the director of my department and Human Resources followed over the next few days, as they tried to figure out what had happened. During the investigation, I said I would not work with this man again, so they moved me to another department. I felt like I was being punished. As far as I knew, there were no repercussions for the man. I felt ashamed, hurt, and anguished, particularly since I was the one who had to change departments.

A few days after I moved to the new area, I heard the man laughing in the hallway, and I fell apart. I began to weep and couldn't stop. I left the building and wept all the way home. I ended up curled in a ball on my bathroom floor, unable to stop crying, on the brink of suicide. I could not understand how God had allowed this to happen. After all I had gone through in life, how could He allow this physical abuse to happen? How could He allow a situation that would trigger such confusion and pain (and, ultimately, serious depression)?

I wailed in my pain—a deep, animal wail from the pit of my stomach. At that moment, I remembered what C.S. Lewis once wrote: "God whispers to us in our joy and screams to us in our pain." I heard a mighty roar of anguish and heard God weep, and I knew He was not happy that this pain had been inflicted on me.

My husband took me to the doctor the next day. I could not stop crying and was afraid I would harm myself if left alone. After I shared what had happened with the physician's assistant, he immediately left the room to get my doctor, who, after hearing what had happened confirmed that I was suffering from PTSD. He immediately put me on antidepressants. I knew I needed help, but the supposed stigma of being on antidepressants bothered me immensely. I didn't want to take them. My doctor, a wonderful Christian man, helped me to understand that the medication would help me get back on my feet.

Still, I suffered. I continued to go to work and prayed constantly, but each time I saw or heard the man who had hit me, I cringed in fear. I thought of quitting many times yet could not do it. God had placed me here: This was my calling. About two months after the incident, I took some time off to go to the Bahamas with my family. I had to get away from the office and the triggers that brought on the PTSD and depression, as I was continuing to have suicidal thoughts.

"God whispers to us in our joy and screams to us in our pain."

My husband and I had to work through a lot, too. He was my protector and had promised to take care of me, yet I had forbidden him to take any action. We talked and came to terms with what had happened. I took many long walks on the beach and spent many silent moments at the edge of the water with God. Many times I felt His presence so strongly that it was as though we were sitting shoulder-to-shoulder, with me sharing and Him listening and understanding my pain. The day before we were to return home, I asked the Lord again to take away the pain and anger and to help me to continue in my job. I was tired of hurting and being angry. I just wanted to go back home and take care of myself and my family, while doing what He had called me to do.

Back at work the following Monday, I was shocked to learn that the man had resigned from his position that very day. God had taken care of things. Still, I wondered why I had had to go through the situation at all. God could have stopped this man from hitting me. He could have prevented me from suffering from PTSD and the depression. Yet He did not. A few weeks later, I knew why.

In my new department and role, I worked on promoting a women's conference and successfully increased attendance at the conference by thousands, over a very short period of time. At the event, I looked at all the women there and saw the difference this conference was making in their lives. I was amazed at God's goodness. I slipped away to the top level of the conference center as the program was ending. It was quiet there, and I wanted to be alone to pray.

As I looked down at the thousands of women, I heard the Lord whisper, "And they came, bringing their hurt, their pain, their disappointments, their sicknesses." He was letting me see Him in each of these women and the healing that He was providing, much as He had provided to me. He showed me that in my weakness and my pain, He had been able to use me to bring hope and healing to thousands of women.

Suddenly, I heard someone crying behind me. I froze for a second, because I had thought I was alone. I turned around slowly and saw a woman standing against the wall, crying. I went over to her and held her in my arms while she wept. I knew and understood the sound of that weeping. I knew it came from a deep place of hurt. As I looked into her face, I offered her words of reassurance. My own recent trial allowed me to comfort this woman.

That is when I realized that God had taken a difficult situation and restored me, making my faith stronger. In other words, what had been meant for evil had been used for good. That woman had prayed for God to show her just one person who cared. She had slipped into that quiet top level away from everyone to weep and pray. God had placed me there, broken but healing, so I could offer her hope. God did care for her. He would make things right for her, as He had for me.

I stayed in my role at the ministry for five and a half years after this incident, still struggling with depression but depending on God to finish the healing. I tried several times to come off the antidepressants but I only lasted a few days before I needed to go back on them. I could see God's healing and strength, though, as I faced other challenges and workday stresses.

In September 2008, I felt God calling me to a new assignment, and so I began to ask God to release me from my assignment at the ministry. I wanted to be sure that what I was feeling was truly from Him. He answered my prayers and made a way for me leave in January 2009, when I was laid off. I had been loyal to the ministry and the work God called me to do, under difficult circumstances. I had chosen obedience to God above my own hurts and I had chosen to honor God with the gifts and talents that He had given me. When I walked out those doors on my last day, I was relieved and held my head up high, knowing I had fulfilled and completed my assignment faithfully. It was also the last day that I had to take an antidepressant.

Perhaps you have suffered a traumatic event in your life that has left you in so much pain that all you can do is think about it day after day, reliving each agonizing moment. I know what that's like. I've been there. That workplace incident tore my world apart, and even though I had forgiven that man, I still battled depression for five years. Yet, those were also the five most successful years of my life. Those were the years when I felt that I was truly living my purpose—that I was doing exactly what God had created me to do. I was fulfilling God's plans for my life. Everything I touched was successful. I knew that in my weakness and battle with depression, God was strong in me, and He was the one really accomplishing everything that I was doing.

Abuse is a terrible thing. It is a hidden scourge in many families and affects society as a whole. According to some estimates, 14 percent of all men and 36 percent of all women in prison in the United States were abused as children, and children who experience child abuse and neglect are 59 percent more likely to be arrested as juveniles. A startling one in three people who have been abused become abusers themselves, continuing a vicious cycle that needs to be broken.

If you have suffered the pain and anguish of abuse, or if this is a hidden sin that has existed in your family for generations, please get professional help and do all you can to break this cycle. This is a generational sin that Satan uses to hold families captive. Free your family and future generations from this curse! Abuse has ruined and will continue to ruin thousands of lives and families if we do not stop it by breaking the cycle. I truly believe that we can turn society around and greatly reduce crime rates by helping victims of abuse and preventing them from becoming abusers themselves.

I believe that a heart that is willing to forgive can break the cycle of abuse that is rampant in our homes and families. Can you imagine how society could change if we all adopted a life of forgiveness and broke all of these vicious cycles that Satan uses to hold families in bondage? Selah! Reflect on that.

The Surrender of Jonah

Scripture reading: The Book of Jonah

The story of Jonah and his sojourn in the belly of a whale because he did not want to obey God and go to the city of Nineveh to tell them to repent is one of the most bizarre stories in the Bible. Yet, it is a story that tells of God's mercy and forgiveness.

When Jonah heard God telling him to go to Nineveh and preach repentance, he refused. Instead he headed in the opposite direction. He found a ship going to Tarshish and bought passage so he could avoid going to Nineveh. But God was not about to let Jonah off so easily. He sent a storm so severe that the mariners were afraid the ship would break up. Finally, by casting lots, the sailors found out that they were going through this mishap because of Jonah. So, Jonah told them to cast him into the ocean. Once the sailors had done so, the sea calmed down.

God protected Jonah from drowning by having a big fish swallow him. Jonah spent three days and three nights in the fish's belly. He was hungry. Cold. And breathing the stinky smell of the fish every second for three days and three nights. It was enough for Jonah to realize that God was serious in His command that Jonah preach repentance to the Ninevites. So Jonah surrendered to God's will and prayed that He would deliver him from the belly of the fish—and God had the fish vomit Jonah onto dry land. This time, when Jonah heard God command him to go and preach His message of repentance to the Ninevites, the people who Jonah considered his enemies, he did as he was commanded. He went to Nineveh and preached, letting the Ninevites know that in forty days, the city would be overthrown if they did not repent. The Ninevites heeded the message, and they all repented. God saw that they had indeed turned away from their evil ways, and He had compassion on them. He relented and did not send the disaster He had said He would send upon them.

However, the Bible says in Jonah 4:1-2, *"But it displeased Jonah exceedingly, and he was very angry. And he prayed unto the Lord, and said, I pray thee, O Lord, [was] not this my saying, when I was yet in my country? Therefore I fled before unto Tarshish; for I knew that thou [art] a gracious God, and merciful, slow to anger, and of great kindness, and repentest thee of the evil."* Jonah did not understand God's compassion for humankind, God's heart for the lost, and God's merciful heart. Jonah was more concerned about himself and his sense of justice. So, in Jonah 4:11 God rebuked Jonah for his unforgiving heart, saying, *"And should not I spare Nineveh, that great city, wherein are more than sixscore thousand persons that cannot discern between their right hand and their left hand; and [also] much cattle?"*

How often do we behave like Jonah? Do we pout instead of rejoicing when God shows mercy and compassion to those who have betrayed us? Do we cry out to God for justice instead of asking God to bless our enemies or those who have hurt us? Can we be Christlike and pray and implore God to forgive and bless those who have wounded us deeply? Or is that too much to hope for?

It is not easy to ask for blessings on those who have hurt us, who have caused a pain so deep that we are almost paralyzed when we try to reach for the dreams God has for us. However, if we want to be free from the hold of Satan and his strategy of continuing to remind us of all the bad things that have happened to us (in order to hold us captive), we need to develop a heart of forgiveness—a heart that is willing to trust God even when we see Him have mercy and pity on those who seem so blatantly undeserving. After all, who are we to question God? Are we more deserving of His mercy and grace than others?

Psalm 103:8-13, shows us who God is, especially towards sinners: *"The Lord [is] merciful and gracious, slow to anger, and plenteous in mercy. He will not always chide: neither will he keep [his anger] for ever. He hath not dealt with us after our sins; nor rewarded us according to our iniquities. For as the heaven is high above the earth, [so] great is his mercy toward them that fear him. As far as the east is from the west, [so] far hath he removed our transgressions from us. Like as a father pitieth [his] children, [so] the Lord pitieth them that fear him."*

———— ∞ ————

A sinner's humanity will cause him to fall from grace again and again, but his human pride, ego, or feeling of unworthiness should not prevent him from seeking God's forgiveness again and again.

———— ∞ ————

God's heart is full of compassion. He never refuses to forgive a sinner if that person comes to Him truly and fully repentant. Once a sinner fully receives and accepts God's forgiveness, his life changes. He then needs to follow God's Commandments and do his best to not sin again. A sinner's humanity will cause him to fall from grace again and again, but his human pride, ego, or feeling of unworthiness should not prevent him from seeking God's forgiveness again and again. To know God and to be in communion with Him, and to have a personal relationship with Jesus Christ as Lord and Savior, should be enough to convict a sinner of God's mercy and compassion, to remind him of God's goodness and love toward him, and to draw him humbly to the foot of the cross seeking God's divine mercy whenever necessary.

So how do we handle it when others sin against us? The Bible tells us in Luke 17:3-4 how we are to behave: *"Take heed to your-selves: If thy brother trespass against thee, rebuke him; and if he repent, forgive him. And if he trespass against thee seven times in a day, and seven times in a day turn again to thee, saying, I repent; thou shalt for-give him."* Just as God forgives us time and time again, we are to offer that same grace and show that same mercy to those who hurt us.

It is not easy, and like Jonah, we may feel a sense of injustice and even anger. But, like Jonah, we need to learn to surrender to God's will and to do what He commands—forgive. In forgiving, we open the door to God's blessings, and we gain redemption for our-selves and also potentially for those who have hurt us.

Part 3

How Can God Forgive Me?

The Forgiveness of David

Scripture readings: Acts 13:22, 1 Kings 14:8, 2 Samuel 11:1-27, 2 Samuel 12:1-24

David is a shining example to us of the way our relationship with God should be. David was devoted to God, he followed God with all his heart, and he put God first. Verse after verse in the Bible speaks of how David was "a man after God's own heart."

In the Bible, we see how David was anointed by God to be king over Israel. He was blessed to win battle after battle, and God protected him from the hand of Saul. He was given his heart's desires. In fact, the Bible says that God would have given him even more, if David had just asked.

But, David sinned.

He was human, just like us. He fell from grace. David committed several sins that were against the word of God. He coveted Bathsheba, another man's wife. Then, he committed adultery with her. Not only did he commit adultery, but when he found out that Bathsheba was pregnant, he orchestrated the death of her husband, Uriah, one of his own soldiers, to hide the fact that he, not Uriah, (who had not slept with his wife for some time) had impregnated Bathsheba.

Premeditated murder.

David was guilty of some serious violations of God's commandments. Where before he had always done what was right in

God's eyes, he had now committed what was evil in God's eyes, as the Bible shows us in 2 Samuel 12:9, *"Wherefore hast thou despised the commandment of the Lord, to do evil in his sight? thou hast killed Uriah the Hittite with the sword, and hast taken his wife [to be] thy wife, and hast slain him with the sword of the children of Ammon."*

However, 2 Samuel 12:13-14 tells us that when Nathan was sent by the Lord to rebuke David, *"...David said unto Nathan," I have sinned against the Lord." And Nathan said unto David, "The Lord also hath put away thy sin; thou shalt not die. Howbeit, because by this deed thou hast given great occasion to the enemies of the Lord to blaspheme, the child also [that is] born unto thee shall surely die."*

David fully accepted the consequence of his sin. He knew that he had blatantly disobeyed God, and so he asked for God's forgiveness and mercy. He still believed in God's goodness to forgive him and to show him mercy. In Psalm 51:10-12, David pleads, *"Create in me a clean heart, O God; and renew a right spirit within me. Cast me not away from thy presence; and take not thy holy spirit from me. Restore unto me the joy of thy salvation; and uphold me [with thy] free spirit."*

David repented and asked for God's mercy and forgiveness and God forgave him. But a consequence of David's terrible sins was the loss of his first son with Bathsheba, the very child that had been conceived through David's lust. This may seem harsh, especially since David had repented and been forgiven. The child, after all, had not done anything wrong. But sin has consequences. Therefore, just because you have been forgiven, it doesn't mean that you will not suffer the consequences. The cost of that sin is for God alone to decide.

But sin has consequences.

Sometimes, we sin against God and then think that because God has forgiven us, we get a free pass and won't incur any consequences for the sin. *But sin has consequences.*

In Hebrews 12:5-7, we learn of God's chastening when we sin: *"And ye have forgotten the exhortation which speaketh unto you as unto children, My son, despise not thou the chastening of the Lord, nor faint when thou art rebuked of him: For whom the Lord loveth he chasteneth, and scourgeth every son whom he receiveth. If ye endure chastening, God dealeth with you as with sons; for what son is he whom the father chasteneth not?"* If we go against the Word of God, we should expect consequences for our sin. We should expect some repercussions. But, we should never forget God's love and compassion…His mercy and grace.

Yet, I have heard people say, "You have no idea what I have done! God would never forgive me." True, I don't know what you have done. But it is not for me to judge. Sin is between an individual and God. There are some things that are really hard to come to terms with—heavy things that people struggle with every day: Abortion. Adultery. Promiscuity. Murder. War atrocities. Stealing. Rape. Dishonoring one's parents.

Perhaps you suffer the burden of PTSD and it has caused you to abuse the family you love. Perhaps you neglected your family because you put ambition and the desire for wealth first, and you lost your family. No matter what it is, you may struggle with all these feelings and emotions, ashamed and burdened by the choices you made and you may wonder, "How can God ever forgive me?"

Here's a thought for you.

If God could forgive David, a man who Acts 13:22 tells us was "a man after God's own heart," for the sins of coveting someone else's wife, adultery and murder—premeditated murder, no less—can God really not forgive you for whatever it is you have done?

David went on to have many blessings in his life after he repented and accepted God's forgiveness. Moreover, God blessed David and Bathsheba with another son, Solomon, who became a great king and built God's temple in Jerusalem, thereby showing His mercy and grace to both David and Bathsheba.

Do you not believe that God wants to show you the same mercy and forgiveness? Are you so blinded by the sin that burdens you that you fail to see the goodness and mercy that God showed David—and that He will show you, also, if you confess your sin and ask God for forgiveness, like David did?

God is merciful. He is just and fair. He is ready to forgive if there is a contrite heart and true repentance. Like David, we have to believe in God's mercy, no matter how many times we fall or sin. Otherwise, we believe in the lies of the evil one rather than the promises of the Holy One, and that is the path to disaster.

Ask yourself again, "If God could forgive David, why would He not forgive me?

The Celebration of the Prodigal Son

Scripture reading: Luke 15:11-32

In the parable of the prodigal son, Jesus talks about a father who had two sons. The younger of the two went to his father and asked his father for his inheritance—the assets that he would normally receive after his father had died. His father, although heartbroken, gave him his inheritance, whereupon the young man left home and went and spent all of it living the high life and spending his father's hard-earned money on prostitutes.

Meanwhile, his elder brother stayed home working in the fields and dutifully taking care of all that his father entrusted to him. He is portrayed as a hard-working man, obedient to his father's wishes.

The younger brother soon exhausted his fortune and became so destitute and so hungry that even the swill that the pigs were eating looked good! He remembered how good a life he had had in his father's home—and realized that even the servants there were fed better than what he was reduced to eating. So, he decided to return and ask for his father's mercy.

But, his father saw him while he was still a great distance from the house and ran to meet him. This heartbroken father must have spent much time watching the horizon, hoping that some day his son would return. So, when he saw his son coming in the distance, he was filled with joy and compassion for him. He could tell that his son had fallen on hard times. Did he ask his son anything? Did his voice or actions condemn him? No. There were no recriminations (although they would have been well-deserved).

There was only love...joy...compassion. The father was so filled with joy at seeing his son that all he wanted to do was hold him and kiss him. He ran and welcomed his son back with open arms. Even when his son asked for his forgiveness and stated that he was no longer worthy to be called his son, the father showed his mercy by telling his servants to bring out the best robe and put it on his son. He had them put a ring on his finger and sandals on his feet. He told them to kill and prepare the fatted calf for a celebration. The father did not humiliate his son. He did not banish him from his sight. He did not criticize him for his sinful living. He did not disinherit him. Instead, he embraced his son. He rejoiced and welcomed him home. He celebrated his return. He affirmed that this undeserving young man was still his son.

This is how God, our Father, celebrates our return when we fall from grace. This is how He receives us when we repent and confess to Him that we have sinned against Him. He waits patiently for us, watching intently for our return. And when we come—humble, repentant and contrite, seeking His forgiveness and mercy—He embraces us. He pours out His love over us. He celebrates our return. He forgives us and forgets all the bad that we have done. He gives us a fresh start.

> There was only love...joy... compassion.

However, there is another part to the parable that is not often talked about—and that is the reaction of the older brother, who was not joyful. Instead, he was angry and judgmental. He refused to join in the celebration, believing that the father had been unfair to him and, in forgiving the younger son, had overlooked the older son's steadfast obedience and faithfulness.

We sometimes do the same, don't we? Instead of being happy when we see someone who has sinned or led a sinful life repent and find their way back to God and His blessings, we judge or resent them. When someone has hurt us or betrayed us, we may wish for them to be punished, to suffer, to incur ill fortune—rather than praying for them to be convicted of God's love and mercy.

We fail to remember that we, too, were once unforgiven sinners. We get greedy and question why God blesses someone else who has led a sinful life and repented—especially if we think they are being blessed more than we are. We forget in that moment how much God has blessed us and will continue to bless us, if we only ask Him. How often do we say to God, "It isn't right!" or "It isn't fair!" when our self-pity becomes judgment, and we believe that we should get more because we are doing all the right things (supposedly)?

We forget in those moments of self-righteous indignation that those people who God is blessing are also children of God. Perhaps if we remembered that, we would be more inclined to celebrate the return to the fold of a lost one than to respond in any kind of negative way when they repent and God blesses them.

After all, when we repent, God forgives us. He celebrates us. He welcomes us back with open arms. There are no recriminations from Him. No anger. No condemnation. Just love. Compassion. Joy. Celebration.

The Bible says in Luke 15:7, "*I say unto you, that likewise joy shall be in heaven over one sinner that repenteth, more than over ninety and nine just persons, which need no repentance.*" Can you picture that? Joy and celebration in heaven over the repentance of every single sinner! That's what God does. He celebrates every single sinner who seeks forgiveness. He embraces each sinner who repents and turns back to Him.

If you are asking yourself, "How can God forgive me?" look to 1 John 1:9, where the Bible tells us how to seek God's forgiveness: "*If we confess our sins, he is faithful and just to forgive us [our] sins, and to cleanse us from all unrighteousness.*" This means acknowledging what we've done wrong, turning toward God and striving to live according to the example set for us by Jesus Christ.

God can and will forgive you. He has too much compassion and love for you to turn you away. Like the father of the prodigal son, He is waiting for you to come to Him in repentance. Don't allow pride to hold you back from seeking God's forgiveness. Don't allow ego to prevent you from seeking God and His mercy. Don't allow a false sense of unworthiness to stop you from a loving relationship with God. Go to Him in humility and acknowledge and turn away from your sins. God is good. He will welcome you back with open arms and a joyous celebration in heaven, just as the Bible promises.

10

The Suffering of Jesus

Scripture reading: Matthew 26:14-75, Matthew 27:1-56, Mark 14:10-72, Mark 15:1-41, Luke 22:14-71, Luke 23:1-49, John 13:1-38, John 18:1-40, John 19:1-37

I recently had the opportunity to view a full-scale replica of the Shroud of Turin. (The original Shroud is kept in the Cathedral of St. John the Baptist in Turin, and is only brought out for viewing on rare occasions. The next public display is scheduled for 2020).

The Shroud is believed to be the burial cloth of Jesus—the cloth in which His body was wrapped after His death before being placed in a tomb. The documented history of the Shroud began in 1353. Since then, many tests have been conducted on the material, pigments and blood on the Shroud to determine whether it is truly the burial cloth of Jesus.

In 1981, after spending three years analyzing data from the Shroud, the scientists who were part of the Shroud of Turin Research Project (STURP) released a statement at an international conference in New London, Connecticut, stating: *"We can conclude for now that the Shroud image is that of a real human form of a scourged, crucified man. It is not the product of an artist. The blood stains are composed of hemoglobin and give a positive test for serum albumin."*

As I stood before that beautiful replica of the Shroud, I was struck by the definition of the wounds on the body captured so clearly on the cloth: the crown of thorns, the scourge marks, the nail wounds in the wrist and feet, and the wound in the side. Then, there were the blood markings that clearly showed each of the wounds on the body of the man who had been wrapped in the cloth. I was overwhelmed by what I was looking at and could not stop the tears that rolled down my face. For the first time in my life, I was faced with the realization of the ultimate price that was paid for my salvation, *in full graphic detail.*

I have read the accounts in the Gospels of Jesus' last hours many, many times, but nothing had prepared me for what I saw, as the full implications of what the Shroud depicts hit me. Perhaps it was the brokenness that I was experiencing at the time—the intense emotional and psychological pain brought on by an act of betrayal by a member of my extended family—that finally allowed me to see what I had not seen before.

Even as you read the Bible, I don't think you fully grasp the reality of what Jesus suffered for each one of us unless you study each chapter and verse of His last days carefully. But, perhaps understanding a little of what Jesus faced and the suffering that He went through is what is needed so one can understand the deep love that God has for each one of us—a love so deep that it allows Him to forgive the most heinous sins…a love that He showed by sending His one and only beloved Son to suffer and die an excruciating death, so that we can have eternal life with Him.

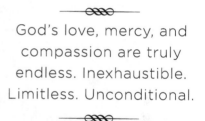

God's love, mercy, and compassion are truly endless. Inexhaustible. Limitless. Unconditional.

God's love, mercy, and compassion are truly endless. Inexhaustible. Limitless. Unconditional.

After seeing the Shroud, I spent quite a bit of time studying the Gospels and letting each part of Jesus' suffering sink into my being. After I had been so blatantly betrayed by the family member,

I found myself kneeling in front of a crucifix, sometimes for hours, just immersing myself in the suffering of Jesus, meditating on the wounds on His body, as I sought to forgive what that family member had done. My knees were black and blue from the hours of kneeling, but I knew that the only place where I would find the courage to forgive was at the foot of the cross. My prayers and meditation led me to an incredible place of understanding, trust, love, and hope.

The Last Supper

Jesus chose to spend His last hours and His last meal with His disciples. Can you imagine the mental torment He must have been going through, knowing that shortly He would be betrayed by one of His very own disciples and denied by another? Yet, He took the time to share that last Passover meal with them, even while knowing that He would soon be undergoing an agonizing and painful death.

He continued to teach them about the new covenant that was about to come to fruition with His death on the cross. He showed them what true servant leadership entailed, by washing their feet. He comforted them and encouraged them to keep the faith and the commandments. He assured them that He was going to prepare a place for them in Heaven. He didn't use His last hours to condemn or criticize them. He spoke truth to them, letting them know that He knew He was about to be betrayed, denied, and led to an excruciating death with few of His disciples by His side. Most of all, He showed His great love for them, even though He knew that their faith in Him would be shaken to the core that very night.

And God does the same for us. No matter how many times we let Him down, no matter how many times we walk away from Him, no matter how many times we sin against Him and break His commandments, God continues to love us. He does not condemn us, but rather, He waits patiently for us to find our way back to Him—and He celebrates each return of a lost one to the fold.

How great is His love for each one of us! Can we emulate that love by forgiving what others do to us? Or can we love ourselves enough to ask for and accept God's forgiveness for the bad decisions we make that separate us from Him?

The Betrayal

Judas betrayed Jesus for thirty pieces of silver. Peter denied Jesus three times. In Matthew 26:56 says, "...*Then all the disciples left Him and fled.*" Jesus faced a betrayal that would lead to His horrific suffering and death by a disciple who had become like family to Him—a disciple who had traveled with Him, seen the miracles, and heard the teachings. Yet, this disciple, Judas Iscariot, had allowed the love of money to subvert his loyalty to Jesus. He had succumbed to the evil leading and deceptions of Satan.

Then, Peter denied knowing Jesus—not once, but three times, as Luke 22:60-61, records "*And Peter said, 'Man, I know not what thou sayest.' And immediately, while he yet spake, the cock crew. And the Lord turned, and looked upon Peter. And Peter remembered the word of the Lord, how he had said unto him, 'Before the cock crow, thou shalt deny me thrice.'*"

Can you imagine the Master's pain, as He heard Peter denying Him? Can you imagine His feeling of abandonment at a time when He needed His disciples, His friends, the most? Can you feel His sorrow?

If you have ever suffered a rejection or betrayal at the hands of a family member or trusted friend, I know that you understand when I say it is one of the most painful psychological and emotional hurts that a person can go through. It drains you of strength. It breaks your heart and shakes you to the very core of your being. It can destroy your faith, depending on how great the betrayal is. It can lead to a lifetime of unforgiveness. It has been known to rip families apart—sometimes causing feuds that can last for generations, if left unresolved and unforgiven.

But if the Master could forgive Peter, when Peter wept and repented, can you not also forgive what was done to you? Can you not let the pain of that betrayal go, so that you can be happy and have the abundant life that Jesus came to ensure for you?

The Agony in the Garden

As Jesus prayed in the Garden of Gethsemane, He began to feel the sorrow and distress of His impending suffering and death. He was not surprised by His upcoming death on the cross. In fact, He knew what was ahead of Him and had probably known for His entire life, as many Scriptures foretold. But the humanity of Jesus was tormented by the suffering ahead. Luke 22:44 says, "*And being in an agony he prayed more earnestly: and his sweat was as it were great drops of blood falling down to the ground.*"

Yet, even as Jesus agonized, even as He prayed to the Father to take away the cup of suffering that He was about to undergo, He also prayed for God's will to be done, even if that meant He had to take the cup of suffering in order to bring salvation, to every person who wants it. Jesus surrendered to the Father's will and obediently took on all the suffering and torment that He needed to endure in order to ensure salvation for each one of us.

Will you trust God with all your pain and suffering? Can you take Jesus' example and say, "This is too painful, Father. However, not my will, but Your will be done. Use my pain and suffering for Your glory." This is difficult for even the most mature believer, and yet, if one learns to trust God with everything, the good and the bad, especially the very difficult and traumatic events in our lives, then unforgiveness will not take root in our hearts—leading to more pain and suffering from illness, anger, bitterness, and a broken relationship with God.

If you learn to trust God with all the trials and tribulations you go through in life, you will not give Satan a stronghold over you. Satan uses unforgiveness in our lives to take us captive and he tries to tell us that God does not love us because He has allowed us to go through trials and tribulations. *This is a lie!* If you take an honest look at the difficult situations that you are experiencing or have experienced, you will see that the situation was caused by a decision that you made, or a decision that someone else made, using the free will that God has given each one of us.

God will test us, as He did with Abraham and Sarah. As He did with Joseph. However, God, in His mercy, even as He allows trials and tribulations in our lives, knows just how He will use those experiences to draw us closer to Him, if we let Him. He knows exactly how He will use our tears and pain to help another person find his or her way to Him. He knows exactly how He will use our suffering to refine us until we reveal the character of Christ.

As Isaiah 48:10 says, *"Behold, I have refined thee, but not with silver; I have chosen thee in the furnace of affliction."*

Trials and tribulations allow God to mold us into who He created us to be. We just have to continue to trust Him when hardships come our way, to lean on Him, and to be Christ-like in surrendering to God's will for us.

The Beating, the Mockery and the Trial

The Bible says in Luke 22:63-65, *"And the men that held Jesus mocked him, and smote [him]. And when they had blindfolded him, they struck him on the face, and asked him, saying, 'Prophesy, who is it that smote thee?' And many other things blasphemously spake they against him."*

> Trials and tribulations allow God to mold us into who He created us to be.

Jesus was beaten savagely, spit on, slapped, sneered at, and ridiculed. He was mocked and treated contemptuously, a crown of thorns was jammed on His head, and He was dressed in a cloak and paraded around in resplendent garb. He went through the farce of a trial, and felt the anguish of hearing the crowd screaming for His crucifixion. Then, after being scourged and tormented, He was stripped naked and crucified in a public place, in front of His mother and closest friend. Imagine the torment. Imagine the humiliation. Imagine the shame.

Yet, not a word of anger or condemnation did He utter. He could have called upon the Father many times to save Him from all of this humiliation and torment, yet He did not do it. Why not? For one reason, and one reason alone: Love. His love for each one of us and His desire to secure eternal salvation for each one of us made Him willing to suffer and lay down His life.

Can we take on that same kind of meekness and continue to trust God when others bully us or treat us as second-class citizens? Can we suffer in silence, without complaining, while waiting for God to vindicate us?

The Crown of Thorns

When Jesus was being mocked as "King of the Jews," a crown of thorns was pressed on His head to cause additional pain. Every movement He made caused the thorns to dig into His head, tearing into His flesh. Blood dripped down His face. Can you see it in your mind's eye? Can you imagine the agony of those thorns digging into the Savior's forehead, pushed even deeper by the blows of the guards? Head wounds tend to bleed profusely. Can you see all that precious blood running down His face?

The Scourging

I was filled with sorrow when I first saw the scourging scene in the Mel Gibson movie, *The Passion of The Christ*. I could not believe the brutality of the scourging, and at one point during that scene, I remember screaming out in my mind, "Stop! Enough already!" I wept openly and publicly in the theater that day.

Typically, the instrument used for flogging was a short whip with several single or braided leather thongs that had pieces of sharp bone or metal tied to the braids. This was an instrument that was designed to bring great injury and pain to the person it was used on. Every lash of the whip burned like fire!

As Jesus was being scourged, the metal would have caused deep bruises all along His back, shoulders, and the backs of His legs, while the sharp pieces of bone ripped and tore His back wide open—leaving it a mass of torn, hanging, bleeding flesh. Think about it: Each lash ripped away His skin, His muscles, and His flesh, then opened up His arteries and capillaries so that He bled heavily.

The pain would have been beyond description. The sight horrific. The bleeding extensive.

Yet, a heavy cross was then placed on His shoulders, and He was expected to carry it up to Calvary. How He must have wanted to scream in agony from the weight of that cross on His torn back! Yet, He didn't speak a word. How weak He must have felt from the loss of blood! Yet, silently, He took that heavy cross upon His shoulders—His torn, lacerated, bleeding, ripped-beyond-recognition shoulders—so that the weight of the cross dug into Him, causing Him excruciating pain, while He began to make His way to Calvary. He did this for you. For me. Carrying each of our sins on His wounded shoulders. To give us hope. To give us salvation. To give us eternal life.

Can you not see the love behind this sacrifice?

The Way of the Cross

One foot forward, step by step. Bent over by the weight of the cross. Each step hurting worse than the other, pain shooting through

His body. Falling down from the weight of the cross. Struggling to get back up again. Disheveled. Unkempt. Blood dripping down His face, down His body, down His legs, and mixing with the dust on His feet. Mixing with the dirt on the ground each time He fell from the weight of that cross and His weakened state from the loss of blood. Precious blood…leaving His body drop by drop.

Yet, He kept going. Stumbling. Tortured. He had one goal in mind, one focus: Obedience to God to pay for our sins. Your sins. My sins. The sins of all races. Different nations. Different colors. Different sins. Similar sins. All paid for by one Savior—Jesus.

Do you remember the way of the cross when you fall? Do you struggle to get up or just give up? Do you remember Jesus' struggle and look to the Father to help you get back on your feet? Do you seek Jesus' face even as you suffer, stumble and fall?

The Crucifixion

Death by crucifixion was reserved by the Romans for the worst criminals. Jesus was not a criminal, and yet that was the death He had to suffer to gain our salvation. His blood had to be poured out for us, so that we could be forgiven.

The Bible says in Ephesians 5:2, *"And walk in love, as Christ also hath loved us, and hath given himself for us an offering and a sacrifice to God for a sweetsmelling savour."* Jesus offered Himself up to the Father as a fragrant sacrifice. What a sacrifice!

Nails, about six to eight inches long, were driven into His wrists, in order to break or crush the large median nerve, sending waves of excruciating pain through Jesus' arms, and rendering them virtually useless for supporting His body on that cross. This forced Jesus to use His back to support Himself on that cross—His lacerated, torn, ripped, shredded back. Imagine the pain that accompanied every breath he took!

His feet were nailed together with a single nail, causing intolerable pain as He had to support His body on that one nail and with His back.

His arms were stretched wide open. Inviting all to come to Him. Welcoming all nations, all races, everyone, and anyone. Forgiving all. Past sins. Present sins. Future sins. For three hours He hung there—fighting to breathe, suffocating slowly, struggling with the pain over every inch of His body, yet courageously bearing it all, in obedience to the Father. A sacrifice. For you. For me. So that we could know the joy of salvation. So we could receive forgiveness from the Father. So that all of our sins could be washed away.

In Matthew 26:53, the Bible records Jesus' earlier words to Satan: *"Thinkest thou that I cannot now pray to my Father, and he shall presently give me more than twelve legions of angels?"* Jesus could have prayed at any time to be released from the brutal suffering and death. After all, He had done nothing to deserve it. But He didn't. He knew that this was what it was going to take to gain salvation and eternal life for each one of us—every person who freely wants it. And so, He freely gave His life for ours. The spear that pierced His side released the blood and water from His body. He gave every drop of blood in His body to free us. With every drop of His blood and every breath of His body, He paid our ransom, and He bought our salvation.

Do you truly understand the meaning of the cross? Can you see what it took to obtain salvation for each one of us? Do you now see the price that was paid to wash clean all the sins of humanity?

Even as He suffered while He hung on the cross, Jesus' last words on the Cross were:

Father, Forgive Them, They Know Not What They Do

Even as He was being crucified, even as He was suffering unbearable pain and torment for something He had not even committed—sin, Jesus was able to focus on those who were hurting Him and to ask the Father to forgive them. (And forgive us, for our sins also put Him on that cross.)

In these words, we see the incredible, unconditional love that Jesus has for us—a divine love that enabled Him to sacrifice Himself for us.

Are you tired of the pain of unforgiveness in your heart? Look at Jesus' example, and ask God to give you the grace and courage to forgive.

Jesus Forgives the Criminal

In Luke 23:43, the Bible says, *"And Jesus said unto him, Verily I say unto thee, today shalt thou be with me in paradise."* Even as He was dying, Jesus was able to give one of the two criminals hanging on either side of Him the hope that even at this last moment, that criminal's sins would be forgiven if he repented. That man then acknowledged who Jesus was, and asked Jesus to remember him when He came into His kingdom. Jesus poured out His grace on the man, assuring him that he would indeed receive salvation.

So many times, we hear people say it is too late for them to receive God's forgiveness because of the way they have lived their lives. Yet St. Cyprian said, *"To him who still remains in this world, no repentance is too late. The approach to God's mercy is open."* **It is never too late.** No matter how sinfully a person has lived, no matter how awful his or her sins, God gives grace and forgiveness if they truly repent of their sins and live differently going forward. Even if the repentance is at the last minute, as one is dying, Jesus forgives.

Repentance requires change—specifically, turning away from sin. One cannot say they repent and then continue to live a life that is outside of God's will and commandments. True repentance requires change, and God can (and will) create a new heart in a person who has truly repented.

Jesus' Concern for His Mother

Even as He was dying, Jesus was filled with concern for His mother and gave her into the care of His disciple John. The tenderness with which Jesus did this, even as He was dying, showed His caring, respect, and love for His mother. If Jesus cared for His mother with such tenderness, do you think He would not show the same compassion, caring, and tenderness for each of us, His sheep? The very people He gave His life up for? Do you think that if you called out to Him for help, He would not come to your assistance?

He has already shown you His great love by dying for you. What more do you need in order to know how much He loves you— that He has paid the ransom to free you from all sin...that He is waiting to have a personal relationship with you once you repent and change? What continues to hold you back?

My God, My God, Why Have You Forsaken Me?

Mark 15:34 says, *"And at the ninth hour Jesus cried with a loud voice, saying, 'Eloi, Eloi, lama sabachthani?' which is, being interpreted, 'My God, my God, why hast thou forsaken me?'"* This was Jesus' darkest hour, the moment when He felt that His Father had abandoned Him. This was the moment when Jesus truly bore the weight of the sins of the world, when He *became* sin. And God turned away from Him. I have often wondered if the Father turned away because He could not bear to see the pain that His Son was going through: the torment, the suffering, and the agony.

I am in no way comparing my pain to God's pain, but as a mother who almost lost a child to illness, I can tell you that the moment when the doctors told me my child might not pull through was one of the most agonizing moments of my life. I remember pleading with God to let her live, even offering my life for hers. Then, finally, I came to that place of trusting God with her life, and

I released her to Him. God, in His mercy allowed her to live, and I am so grateful that He did. I am aware of His mercy and also aware of the pain that other parents who have lost children live with every day.

Can you imagine God's pain at seeing His Son on that cross? Tortured? Suffering? In agony? Sacrificing Himself for humanity? Can you see God's ultimate sacrifice—His Son's life—to save each of us?

The Bible says in Deuteronomy 31:6, *"Be strong and of a good courage, fear not, nor be afraid of them: for the Lord thy God, he [it is] that doth go with thee; he will not fail thee, nor forsake thee."* That is God's promise to us: He will *never* leave us nor forsake us. No matter how difficult the situation we may find ourselves in, no matter how tough a trial or tribulation, He never leaves us. We just have to keep believing, trusting and leaning on His promises as He leads us through the dark valley.

I Am Thirsty

In John 19:28, the Bible says, *"After this, Jesus knowing that all things were now accomplished, that the scripture might be fulfilled, saith, 'I thirst.'"*

Jesus knew that the end was near. He refused the vinegar when He was offered it to ease His suffering, as He knew He had to go through everything in order to cleanse us of our sins. Now, with the end imminent, He asked for a drink so that the Scriptures could be fulfilled. "I thirst." Simple words. Christ thirsted for us. Do you thirst after Him the same way He thirsts after you?

It Is Finished

The Bible says in John 19:30, *"When Jesus therefore had received the vinegar, he said, It is finished: and he bowed his head, and gave up the ghost."* Jesus said "It is finished"—meaning that His earthly mission had been completed. His pain and suffering came to an end. His obedience to the Father had been perfect. He had paid for every one of our sins, in fulfillment of the Scriptures. He had become sin, our sin, and paid the price that was required. As a result, we each have been redeemed.

So, are you still holding on to unforgiveness? Are you still believing in the lie that you do not deserve Christ, that you are unworthy? The truth is that all have sinned. None are worthy. Yet each beating, each blow, every bit of mockery, and each step that Jesus took on that way to the cross said, "You are worthy." Each drop of blood He lost said, "You are loved." And, finally, His crucifixion—being nailed to the cross, hanging on the cross for hours, thirsting, struggling to breathe, and His last words—said, "Your sins have been paid for. Your salvation has been assured—bought and paid for—with My blood, My suffering, My life. You are free!"

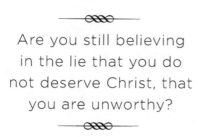

Are you still believing in the lie that you do not deserve Christ, that you are unworthy?

Yet, some still doubt.

We sin against God and doubt His great mercy for us. We believe Satan's lie when he tells us that God cannot forgive us. We believe Satan when he tells us that we are not good enough or worthy enough of God's love. What a travesty!

It's bad enough when we sin against God, but I believe it's a tragedy when we see all that He has done to forgive us—allowing His only beloved Son to die such a tortuous death in order to cleanse humanity of sins—and yet we believe that God is so lacking in love, mercy, grace, compassion, and just pure goodness toward us, that He would hold our sins against us forever.

In Romans 8:38-39, the Bible says, *"For I am persuaded, that neither death, nor life, nor angels, nor principalities, nor powers, nor things present, nor things to come. Nor height, nor depth, nor any other creature, shall be able to separate us from the love of God, which is in Christ Jesus our Lord."* No matter how many times you fall, no matter how heinous the sins you have committed, there is nothing that can keep you from God's mercy and redemption, *if you repent and change.* You can trust in God's divine mercy.

"Why?" you may ask.

Because of this simple truth: God loves you. Period.

John 10:10 records that Jesus said, *"The thief cometh not, but for to steal, and to kill, and to destroy: I am come that they might have life, and that they might have [it] more abundantly."* Life. Abundant life. That's what Jesus came to give us. He came to free us from our sins by taking our sins upon Himself and paying the ultimate price for them in order to secure the ultimate gift: Salvation. Eternal life.

So, if you believe that Jesus came to free us from our sins and give us abundant life, why are you refusing to accept God's forgiveness, or holding on to unforgiveness?

Here's another thought to ponder: *By **not** accepting God's forgiveness for whatever sin is burdening you, are you saying that Jesus died for nothing?*

All that suffering on the cross—was it all for nothing? Do you realize that even if you were the only person on Earth, God would have still sent His one-and-only Son to die that horrific death on the cross so that you might have eternal life?

Do you know why? It's simple. Because God loves you. **GOD LOVES YOU. PERIOD.**

He *chooses* to love you. He *chooses* to forgive you. He *chooses* to bless you and call you His own. Once you fully grasp that and fully accept the depth and height and width of that love, you have no choice but to fall on your knees and acknowledge what is keeping you away from an incredible relationship with God and His Son, to repent fully, to humbly ask for God's forgiveness, and to accept the consequence of your sin. After that, you must let go and move on in life, accepting and enjoying God's abundant blessings while living a life that trusts God in good times and tough times alike.

If there is one thing that I have learned from my experiences in battling unforgiveness, it is this: God sees our sin, but because He loves us, He chooses to forgive us and take us back each time we fall. But we have to repent, and we have to accept the consequences of our sin. And we have to focus on living our life in accordance with God's commandments—our roadmap for living a holy life according to God's will and purpose for each one of us.

In Luke 22:15, Jesus said to His disciples, *"With desire I have desired to eat this Passover with you before I suffer."* Jesus *desired* to eat that last supper with his disciples. He chose to be with them and spend His last few hours with them, knowing full well that He was going to suffer and die an excruciating death very soon.

That is how much God desires to be with us—He seeks us, earnestly and deeply. He doesn't need to; after all he is the Almighty, the Alpha and the Omega. He chooses us and He chooses to love us, even when we are unworthy of His love. But we have to repent and ask for His forgiveness. We still have to experience certain "logical consequences" of our sin, and we must work hard to not repeat the sin, but God chooses to forgive us when we repent.

What is stopping *you* from accepting God's full forgiveness? I encourage you to pray and meditate on the following questions:

1. I need to ask God to forgive me for

_____.

2. I need to forgive myself for

_____.

3. I need to forgive

_____

(*add the name of someone you need to forgive*) for

_____.

(*add the reason why*).

As you meditate, I encourage you to really look at Jesus and His death on the cross, a death that He took upon Himself so that we could be free from our sins and live the abundant lives that He came to give us. I pray that you remember the sacrifices He made for you. I pray that you are so filled with what that sacrifice means that you will take the hand that Christ is holding out to you, and you will let Him raise you up.

Let this be the day you heal. Let this be the day when you say, "Father, no more. I do not want to hold on to this pain, this doubt, this anguish, and this unforgiveness. I give it all to you. Today, I accept your forgiveness fully. Today, I choose freely to fully forgive all those who have hurt me."

Let this be the day you let go of whatever is stopping you from having that awesome relationship that God wants—no, DESIRES to have with you.

My hope is that as you work through the questions above, you realize you do not need to be separated from God. Whatever has held you captive—whether for a week, a month, a year, or many years—can be easily broken as you yield yourself to God. He can and will create a new heart in you, if you ask Him for the grace and the courage to forgive.

Part 4

Forgiveness

The Redemption of Naomi

Scripture reading: The Book of Ruth

The Book of Ruth is a story of redemption. It is the story of a young woman from Moab, Ruth, whose love and devotion to her Israelite mother-in-law, Naomi, would lead to redemption and a lineage to King David and Jesus.

Naomi was married to Elimelech, and together they had two sons, Mahlon and Chilion. The family moved from Judah to Moab due to a famine that had struck the land. Then, Elimelech passed away leaving Naomi a widow. Mahlon and Chilion married two women from Moab—Ruth and Orpah respectively. Unfortunately, the two men also passed away, leaving all three women widows.

Grieving and without financial means, Naomi decided to return to Judah to her family and released her daughters-in-law from any obligation to remain with her. Orpah tearfully returned to her family, but Ruth showed her love for Naomi by refusing to leave her, as Ruth 1:16-17 says, *"And Ruth said, Intreat me not to leave thee, [or] to return from following after thee: for whither thou goest, I will go; and where thou lodgest, I will lodge: thy people [shall be] my people, and thy God my God: Where thou diest, will I die, and there will I be buried: the Lord do so to me, and more also, [if ought] but death part thee and me."*

Ruth was selfless…kind…and compassionate. Ruth knew how much Naomi was struggling, and refused to leave her. Unfortunately,

Naomi did not see this as God's care for her. Instead, when she returned home and her relatives welcomed her back joyfully, she showed her anger and bitterness at God by saying, "Do not call me Naomi (which means pleasant); call me Mara (which means bitter), for the Almighty has dealt very bitterly with me." In Ruth 1:21, she continued, *"I went out full, and the Lord hath brought me home again empty: why [then] call ye me Naomi, seeing the Lord hath testified against me, and the Almighty hath afflicted me?"*

How often like Naomi, do we look at the hard things that we go through in life as afflictions from God's hands? How many times do we believe Satan's lies and deceptions and blame God—becoming angry at Him, turning our faces away from Him and, sometimes, even walking away from Him? How often do we look at the everyday difficulties of life as God not giving us the dreams and desires of our hearts and, then, turn against Him, not stopping to think that perhaps He has other plans, better plans, for us?

But even though Naomi had hardened her heart against Him, God did not desert her. He did not forget her. He redeemed her through Ruth.

In order for them to survive, Ruth gleaned barley from the fields, walking behind the reapers and picking up the grain that fell to the ground. It was hard work, but she did not complain. She ended up in the fields that belonged to Boaz, a relative of Naomi's husband, Elimelech. That was not a coincidence. That was God providing for Ruth and Naomi.

Boaz noticed Ruth and asked about her. He learned who she was and how she had been kind and faithful in taking care of Naomi. His heart was touched that she had left her home and her parents and come with Naomi in order to care for her. He ordered his workers to let her glean even from the sheaves and to let extra grain fall purposefully so that Ruth could gather plenty for herself and Naomi. Through a series of fascinating events, Boaz was able to take responsibility for Ruth and Naomi. He married Ruth and they had a son, Obed, who became the father of Jesse, who in turn was the father of David.

The Bible says in Ruth 4: 14-15, *"And the women said unto Naomi, Blessed [be] the Lord, which hath not left thee this day without a kinsman, that his name may be famous in Israel. And he shall be unto thee a restorer of [thy] life, and a nourisher of thine old age: for thy daughter in law, which loveth thee, which is better to thee than seven sons, hath born him."* This was confirmation for Naomi that God had never left her. It was affirmation that God had provided for her, even when she could not see His face through her sorrow and pain. It was proof for Naomi that even though she had been bitter at her circumstances and blamed God, He had not left her. He had not abandoned her. He had ensured her provision even to her old age.

> ...when we do not forgive and carry the bitterness of unforgiveness in our hearts, we create a barrier between us and God.

So many times when we do not forgive and carry the bitterness of unforgiveness in our hearts, we create a barrier between us and God. This prevents us from receiving all of God's blessings. Naomi would have missed out on being an ancestral "in law" (through Ruth) of Jesus if she had forced Ruth to leave her alone. She was saved from this loss by the selfless love and compassion of Ruth, who was determined to take care of her mother-in-law because it was the right thing to do. It didn't matter that she would be a foreigner in Judah. Indeed, she became the instrument through which God redeemed Naomi. And God rewarded Ruth by giving her a good and just man for her husband—Boaz. A man who also believed in doing the right thing by taking over the responsibility for Ruth and Naomi, because he was a distant relative of Naomi's husband.

God says in Jeremiah 29:11, *"For I know the plans that I have for you," declares the LORD, "plans to prosper you and not to harm you, plans to give you hope and a future."* This is God's promise to us—a promise of hope, blessing, and abundant life. When we do not let go of past sins and do not accept God's forgiveness, or do not forgive what others have done to us, we shackle ourselves to those events that hold us captive. We cannot move beyond those events and therefore prevent ourselves from receiving God's blessings in our lives. We fall short of living our purpose, ever reaching our full potential, or fulfilling our greatest work for God's glory.

When life happens and things do not go the way we want or would like, we have to be careful about letting anger seep into our hearts—anger at God for lost dreams and desires, anger at others for the wrong that they have done to us, and anger at ourselves for our failures. Anger is a tool of the devil. It is an instrument that he uses to keep us from receiving all the blessings that God has planned for us. It is a device that he uses to make us turn away from God, to blind us to God's pure goodness and goodwill toward us.

Confusion is another tool that Satan uses to manipulate us. Naomi could not understand how God could allow her to lose all the men in her life, the men who would be able to take care of her and provide for her. Her mind was clouded with grief and pain, and she blamed God. In 1 Corinthians 14:33, the Bible says, *"For God is not [the author] of confusion, but of peace, as in all churches of the saints."* God is not the author of confusion. God is not a God of rejection, shame, or guilt. Satan adds confusion, shame, guilt, and rejection to your life in order to abort the blessings that God has planned for you. God rewarded Ruth (and Naomi through Ruth) with a good husband and a son. He rewarded Ruth's faithfulness, loyalty, and suffering. He rewarded her more than she could ever ask for—by allowing her, a foreigner, to be the great grandmother of David—and thus, an ancestor of Jesus Christ.

Are you angry at God? Is there something in your life that has you asking "Where are you, God?" Are you in the throes of suffering and blinded to God's love and plans for your life? Have you been caught up in the devil's lies and deceptions about God's plans for you? Stand strong in your suffering. Forgive if you need to. Seek God's forgiveness if that is what is holding you in bondage. Most of all, trust God.

Like Ruth, you will be rewarded in God's timing for your faithfulness.

The Courage of Esther

Scripture reading: The Book of Esther

Courage. Fear. God's providence. God's protection on His people. These are the themes of the Book of Esther. It tells the story of a young Jewish orphan, Esther, living in the Persian Empire, and raised by her uncle, Mordecai, after her parents died. Due to her beauty, Esther ended up in the king's harem when he was searching for a new queen. She became the king's favorite above all the other women in the harem, and thus became queen.

But Haman, the king's chief advisor, concocted a plot to destroy all the Jews because he was angry that Mordecai would not bow to him and pay him homage as had been commanded by the king. So, Haman obtained the King's permission to annihilate the Jews.

Mordecai, after learning of this decree, sent word to Esther letting her know of the decree to kill all the Jews. He asked her to go before the king and ask for the deliverance of her people. Esther sent word back to Mordecai that she could not just go into the king's presence without being summoned—that doing so could mean immediate execution. Mordecai replied to Esther (4:14), *"For if thou altogether holdest thy peace at this time, [then] shall there enlargement and deliverance arise to the Jews from another place; but thou and thy father's house shall be destroyed: and who knoweth whether thou art come to the kingdom for [such] a time as this?"*

Esther showed a courage beyond her years and a willingness to die for her people, in her response to Mordecai in Esther 4:16, saying, *"Go, gather together all the Jews that are present in Shushan, and fast ye for me, and neither eat nor drink three days, night or day: I also and my maidens will fast likewise; and so will I go in unto the king, which [is] not according to the law: and if I perish, I perish."*

Trembling, heart pounding, and terrified, Esther headed for the throne room. Fully aware that she could be put to death for approaching the king without being summoned, Esther courageously waited for the king to notice her. And he did. He extended the golden scepter in his hand and gave Esther permission to stand before him and make her request. Ultimately, Esther's courage in the face of fear foiled Haman's plot and saved her people.

So many times in life, we fail to act on wonderful opportunities that God has planned for us by hesitating, or because of fear. Fear of the unknown. Fear of failure. Fear of ridicule. Looking back over my life, as I've pondered Esther 4:14, I can see the times when I could have done things differently, or taken a different path. While I have no regrets for how my life has turned out, sometimes I feel pain that I did not always take the path that God had marked out for me—especially when I failed to follow the path of forgiveness. But, I have learned from those mistakes.

As Mordecai told Esther, God would raise up others to deliver the Jews if she did not step up to the plate, but he also told her that this may well have been her calling for that particular time. God calls us to certain opportunities, and He gives us the free will to decide whether we will answer the call or decline. He gives us the free will to seek and accept His forgiveness or not. He gives us the free will to choose courageously to forgive those who have hurt us or traumatized us…or not to forgive. It is our choice, our decision alone, whether to obey and follow.

I know that I may not ever stand before a king like Esther, but someday, I will kneel before my Lord and Savior Jesus, my King. When that day comes, I want to kiss those nail-scarred feet and hear Him whisper, "Well done, good and faithful servant." I want to have a heart like Jesus, a heart that is forgiving even in the face of the most sorrowful adversity. Even in the face of loss that I cannot understand. Even in the face of pain and hurt that threatens to suffocate the very life out of me. Still, I will pray for the courage to forgive—the courage of Esther.

———∞———

...a heart like Jesus, a heart that is
forgiving even in the face of the most
sorrowful adversity.

———∞———

What about you? Is God calling you to forgive something that you are hesitating about? Is your conscience urging you to seek His forgiveness?

May you have the courage of Esther to pursue whatever it is that God is calling you to do.

13

What is Forgiveness?

In the dictionary, the word "forgive" means to cease to feel resentment against one's enemies. I believe that forgiveness is more than just forgiving one's enemies. I believe it is a difficult journey—one that includes praying for God's blessings on those who have betrayed us, whether family, friends, colleagues, or even strangers. It means releasing those who we trusted with our love and friendships, yet who have left us bruised and broken…the very people who should have cared for us, but instead wounded and scarred us, making it difficult for us to move toward other trusting relationships or fulfilling lives.

But as Mahatma Gandhi once said, "The weak can never forgive. Forgiveness is the attribute of the strong."

I believe that forgiveness is a way of life, an act of love, and a choice that requires strength and courage for:

(1) daily forgiveness of self—asking God to forgive us, receiving and accepting God's forgiveness, and

(2) daily forgiveness of those who hurt us.

I think Mark Twain put it best when he said, "Forgiveness is the fragrance the violet sheds on the heel that has crushed it." The visual of those words is powerful. Imagine the violet flower—beautiful, pure, and innocent—until a thoughtless person crushes the violet with his heel. Yet the response of the violet is to release a beautiful fragrance that fills the air and covers the foot that crushed it. We can be like that violet in the way we respond to offenses committed against us. We do not have any control over the circumstances that may wound us, but we can control how we react to those difficult circumstances, and we can forgive if we so choose.

Forgiveness is repentance.

Psalm 32:5 says, "*I acknowledged my sin unto thee, and mine iniquity have I not hid. I said, I will confess my transgressions unto the Lord; and thou forgavest the iniquity of my sin.*"

Repentance is about changing your way of life once you have been forgiven and have accepted God's forgiveness and grace. It is about living in a way that is pleasing to God and understanding and knowing that when you fall from grace, God will forgive you when you repent and come to Him with a contrite heart seeking forgiveness. It is about forgiving others, especially when they ask for your forgiveness and show true remorse and change of heart.

It means giving up our rebellious ways and forgiving those who have hurt us. Unforgiveness is rebellion against God's Word, as we are commanded to forgive. It is not an easy mandate to follow, just as obeying the Ten Commandments is not easy, but that is what our foundation of faith and belief is as Christians.

Forgiveness is humility.

It means being humble enough to face yourself and God daily and to be able to say, "Father, I am sorry for failing You, but with Your grace, I will try my best to not sin again."

In Micah 6:8, the Bible says, "*He hath shewed thee, O man, what [is] good; and what doth the Lord require of thee, but to do justly, and to love mercy, and to walk humbly with thy God?*" It means being humble enough to forgive someone else for the wrong they have done to you. Humility brings forth repentance, repentance opens the heart to forgiveness, and forgiveness opens the door to receiving God's blessings.

Forgiveness is meekness.

It is about not putting yourself above someone else, or thinking that you are better than someone else, and therefore wanting them to come and beg for your forgiveness. It is about not letting shame hold you captive. It is about rising above any shame or fear of rejection to ask for and accept God's forgiveness, to forgive yourself or forgive an injury from another person. Forgiveness is about being okay with not getting that apology or that "sorry" from someone who has hurt you, because they are too ashamed to apologize. Be strong and forgive them anyway as this releases blessings from heaven!

Forgiveness is perseverance.

It is about understanding that you will fall and let God down, but it is about getting up again and daily asking God to forgive you and to give you the strength and courage to keep going. Don't let Satan hold you down with his lies when he whispers that God cannot forgive what you have done. Jesus calls us to persevere in John 16:33 saying, *"These things I have spoken unto you, that in me ye might have peace. In the world ye shall have tribulation: but be of good cheer; I have overcome the world."*

Christ died for our sins and has paid the ransom in His blood to pay for all of our sins, no matter how dreadful or horrible they are. We honor God by persevering, by believing in His goodness to forgive us and by working hard to not sin again. It is about persevering during those tough times of struggle when we have been hurt. It is about trusting God even when we question why He has allowed a horrible hardship to come into our life.

Forgiveness is faith.

In Psalm 34:19, the Bible says, *"Many [are] the afflictions of the righteous: but the Lord delivereth him out of them all."* Faith is about believing even when we cannot see God in the midst of our pain. It is about believing in Him—especially when times are tough. It is about resting in the knowledge that no matter how painful the situation you face, He is working to give you grace and transform you through it.

Forgiveness is trust.

It is about trusting God with all your pain, hurt, and sorrow that He has allowed into your life, knowing that He will use it for good. In 2 Timothy 4:17, the Bible says, *"Notwithstanding the Lord stood with me, and strengthened me."*

There is not a single tear that is shed, not a pain or sorrow that is felt, that God does not use for His glory. Even as you go through it, He already knows how, what, when, and where those tears, pain, and sorrow will be used, and He strengthens you.

Forgiveness is surrender.

It is about surrendering to God's mercy and grace when we fail. It is about surrendering to God's will when a hardship comes into our life. It is about surrendering our pain, sorrow, and heartache to God when someone else hurts us, and not seeking revenge on that person.

Forgiveness is acceptance.

It is about accepting the consequences of our sin, even as we accept God's forgiveness. It is about standing on the promise that nothing can keep us or separate us from the love of God (Romans 8:28-29). It is acceptance of God's grace and mercy.

Forgiveness is celebration.

It is about celebrating the life of forgiveness that we choose to live. It is about celebrating God's forgiveness for something we have done. It is about being set free from sin by God's grace and living the life of redemption and blessing that comes from forgiveness. It is about forgiving others and seeing them be set free from their shame, and return to a closer communion with God and a deeper relationship with Jesus. It is the freeing knowledge that we are no longer held captive by Satan's lies.

Forgiveness is suffering.

There is suffering that comes with forgiveness. It is about sacrificing all the hurt, pain, and sorrow that we have experienced, so that we can be free—truly free. It is about putting all that pain, sorrow, and hurt in God's hands and letting go. Forgiveness is painful; it's hard because it goes against the human desire to have justice or even revenge for the wrongs done to us. However, when we forgive each person who has hurt us deeply, we are able to take back the power over our life. It's like saying, "Yes, you chose to hurt me. You made the decision to do whatever it was you did to inflict much pain and sorrow on me. But, I forgive you, not because you deserve it, but because I deserve to be happy. I will not allow you to hold me captive for the rest of my life because of what you chose to do to me."

So, take back the power over your life. Don't let someone else's wrong actions continue to occupy your mind and wound your heart by failing to forgive them.

When you find yourself struggling to forgive what someone has done to you, look at them as being God's child too. See their sin against you as Satan's manipulation of them and their weaknesses. You may be surprised at how your heart softens and forgives their transgressions.

Everyone will have a season of suffering of some sort or another, at one time or another. Some suffer more than others. Others suffer less. Job persevered through his suffering, never giving up hope, and always praising God—and God gave him back twice as much as he had lost. Joseph believed in God through all of his trials and tribulations, and God made him a powerful leader, second only to Pharaoh. Ruth and Naomi suffered great losses, yet God blessed their suffering through Boaz's marriage to Ruth, who became the great-grandmother of King David and a direct ancestor of Jesus.

We don't need to question God about our suffering or ask why. C.S. Lewis said, "God, who foresaw your tribulation, has specially armed you to go through it, not without pain but without stain." Sometimes our suffering develops the very best in us and brings about our greatest works or successes. We just have to stand on God's promises of grace to see us through.

Forgiveness is hope.

It is the ability to wait in "confident expectation of good." God's goodness. God's mercy. God's unfailing love. We must not grow faint in the face of adversity, but wait with hopeful anticipation and trust that if God has allowed a season of suffering in our life, then He will somehow use the pain, sorrow, and tears for His glory. Nothing is wasted.

Forgiveness is redemption.

It is about letting God redeem you once you have truly sought His forgiveness or forgiven someone else. It is about allowing God to use your situation for His glory. It is about living a life that shows God's redeeming grace—a life that is free of anger, bitterness, and unforgiveness. It is about seeing yourself—your pain, sorrow, and hurt—as part of God's bigger story. Who you are in Christ, what you believe you are in Christ, and who Christ is in you will determine your ability to forgive.

Forgiveness is courage.

It is about being able to forgive yourself for the biggest failures in your life. It is about being able to forgive even the most traumatic hurt or betrayal by a loved one, a colleague, or even a stranger. It is about having the courage to forgive, even when you don't want to. All because that is what God calls us to do.

Forgiveness does not mean that you condone or agree with what has been inflicted on you. What it does mean is you are making a choice—a courageous decision to forgive. That choice lies with you and you alone. No one can force you to do it. God has given you free will, and that means that the ability or the choice to forgive, or not, is yours.

In Matthew 6:14-15, the Bible states clearly what the repercussions are for not forgiving others, "*For if ye forgive men their trespasses, your heavenly Father will also forgive you: But if ye forgive not men their trespasses, neither will your Father forgive your trespasses.*"

As Christians, we have a mandate to forgive as described in Matthew 5:43-45, "*Ye have heard that it hath been said, Thou shalt love thy neighbour, and hate thine enemy. But I say unto you, Love your enemies, bless them that curse you, do good to them that hate you, and pray for them which despitefully use you, and persecute you; That ye may be the children of your Father which is in heaven: for he maketh his sun to rise on the evil and on the good, and sendeth rain on the just and on the unjust.*" That is our mandate, but nobody can force you to obey it. It is each person's choice to follow or not.

However, ponder these questions for a moment.

Are you willing to take the consequences of a life without God because of unforgiveness? Are you willing to allow someone else to steal away that precious eternal relationship with God, because you are not willing to forgive?

Forgiveness does not mean that you have to be friends with the person who has hurt you or could continue to hurt you if you stay in the relationship. Sometimes, you have to walk away from a friendship or relationship that is destructive to your well-being. But consider this.

Could you help save another person by forgiving them and giving them an opportunity at redemption?

Doctors, psychologists, and counselors confirm that if we hold onto animosity or grudges, these feelings only take away from the peace, happiness, and health of the hurting or offended person—not the offender.

During an address at Earl's Court in London, Dr. R. T. Kendall talked about the deep hurt he experienced while working at Westminster Abbey. He recounted sharing with his dear friend Josef Tson what he was feeling about his situation, and quoted what Josef said to him after he was done speaking.

"You must *totally* forgive them," Joseph Tson said, "for until you totally forgive them, you will be in chains. Release them, and you will be released."

There are two key thoughts here that show what forgiveness truly is:

1. "Total forgiveness" means complete forgiveness. It means pardoning the person who has hurt you beyond anything you ever imagined. It means forgiving the inexcusable. It means digging deep and calling out to the Lord to give you the strength and courage and grace to forgive your offender. Once you have received that deeper grace to forgive, it means letting go.

2. "Release the offender from all the hurt and harm they have inflicted on you because until you do, you will be held in chains." You have to let go: otherwise you will be a captive to the event that was inflicted on you. When you release the person who has offended you through forgiveness, you free yourself.

After being released from a prison where he had been held for twenty-seven years, Nelson Mandela said, "As I walked out the door toward the gate that would lead to my freedom, I knew if I didn't leave my bitterness and hatred behind, I'd still be in prison."

Forgiveness allows you to free yourself from becoming a victim of anger and bitterness. You free yourself from depression and unhealthy relationships. I can attest to this: I went through many health problems because of built-up anger and pain, when I faced my physical and emotional traumas while working at the ministry. It affected my mental health because I was not able to let go of the hurt right away. I became afraid and could not sleep or eat properly.

I remember one night, shortly after the incident with the male coworker, when my youngest daughter came into my bedroom to tell me she wasn't feeling well. She placed her hand on my shoulder to let me know she was there—a gesture that all my kids used when they needed me. That time, however, I woke up from a troubled sleep, screaming and I lashed out at her. I thought she was the man who had hurt me. That incident at the ministry cost me five years of my life to depression. It was only when I had totally surrendered and prayed for the man who had hurt me, and forgave him, that I was able to find peace and contentment.

I can now live through the notable dates that marked a significant trauma—April 8, for example, the day I was brutalized—like any other day, without any trepidation or fear, because I was able to let go.

Forgiveness is a process that can sometimes take years to finally heal, depending on the trauma and depth of the offense. Jesus was serious when He told Peter we had to forgive our brothers not seven times, but seventy times seven. He knew that forgiveness was not an easy process, and that there would be days when all the pain and anguish from a particular situation would come to mind again. But, with much prayer and surrendering to God, those wounds will heal.

Choose to forgive! Make that courageous decision, because until you do, you will be held in bondage by that event and you will not experience the incredible life that God has planned for you. You will not be able to receive the many blessings that He has planned for you. You will never fully know His plans for you—plans to prosper you and give you a life of hope. God has given each one of us a gift that no one else has and you will not find out what that is if you hold onto anger and bitterness, if you do not free yourself from the burdens and anguish that hold you captive. If you do not forgive you will never reach your greatest potential. Who knows? Perhaps God's plan for you is to raise you up like Esther to leadership. But you're held back because you have not forgiven someone, and an opportunity for greatness is lost. Or, maybe you are destined to be the next great medical researcher and God's plan for you is to be the one who discovers the cure for cancer or AIDS. But, you are in bondage to an event that you just can't let go of. Or, maybe you are meant to be the best mother or father to the most incredible children, and you fail because you have not let go of the past, and therefore you are crushed by depression.

I am humbled that God's plan for me was to work on a project that saved 63,000 babies from abortion. Had I not forgiven that man, I never would have known the joy of seeing the pictures of some of those babies' faces and knowing that I had played a small part in saving their lives. To God alone be the glory!

As you read this, you may be saying, "You do not know what you are asking me to do" and I say to you, "No, I do not know the suffering that you have endured and continue to endure. I do know how hard it is to forgive. I didn't want to forgive the man who brutally traumatized me. But, I also knew that I did not like the angry, bitter person I was becoming. I could not love God with all my heart and soul the way we are commanded to love God, as part of my heart was taken up with the anger and bitterness that was seeping into my heart. I was not going to give that man that much power over my life, or my love for God, so when I heard God tell me I had to forgive that man, much as I hated it, I did forgive him.

In doing that, and surrendering the pain and hurt to God, I discovered that He can and does give you the grace and courage you need and fills you with the Holy Spirit who will allow you to forgive the most heinous of acts inflicted upon you. You just have to surrender to Him and ask Him for the grace you need. Are you struggling to forgive someone for what they did to you? Ponder these questions:

1. What family or relationship situation do I need to forgive?

2. How can I pray for them?

3. Then, write a letter to the person who has hurt you. Tell the person: What they did. How you felt. How you will be praying for them and asking God to bless them.

4. DO NOT MAIL THE LETTER

Do not pray for harm to befall the person who has hurt you. Instead, pray for God to truly bless the person.

In Colossians 3:12-21, the Bible says, *"And so, as those who have been chosen of God, holy and beloved, put on a heart of compassion, kindness, humility, gentleness and patience; bearing with one another, and forgiving each other, whoever has a complaint against anyone; just as the Lord forgave you, so also should you. And beyond all these things [put on] love, which is the perfect bond of unity. And let the peace of Christ rule in your hearts, to which indeed you were called in one body; and be thankful. Let the word of Christ richly dwell within you, with all wisdom teaching and admonishing one another with psalms [and] hymns [and] spiritual songs, singing with thankfulness in your hearts to God. And whatever you do in word or deed, [do] all in the name of the Lord Jesus, giving thanks through Him to God the Father. Wives, be subject to your husbands, as is fitting in the Lord. Husbands, love your wives, and do not be embittered against them. Children, be obedient to your parents in all things, for this is well-pleasing to the Lord. Fathers, do not exasperate your children, that they may not lose heart."*

This is one of the roadmaps that God has given us to live holy lives as Christians. Forgiveness is a mandate.

Will you follow it? Or, will you choose not to?

14

The Steps to Forgiveness

Unforgiveness usually happens when a person feels that they have been humiliated, deceived, abused, or betrayed by another person. A trust is broken, and atonement has not taken place. The incident has not been made right. Apologies have not been extended. Other times, we put a protective barrier around ourselves to hide those wounds that are deep within us—wounds caused by abuse, neglect, or just plain malice. Those sins that are hidden in families for fear of shame or more harm. Then, there are those issues of unforgiveness that stem from lost or shattered dreams—issues that lead us to distance ourselves from God because of our anger toward Him.

In Matthew 18:21-22, Peter came to Jesus and asked, *"Lord, how oft shall my brother sin against me, and I forgive him? till seven times?" Jesus saith unto him, "I say not unto thee, Until seven times: but, Until seventy times seven."* I often thought about this verse during the anguish that I went through after the physical abuse incident at the ministry. How was I supposed to forgive that man? I couldn't bring myself to forgive him once, let alone seventy times seven! Fortunately, this incident happened during Lent. Easter is one of my favorite times of the year in the church, and even as I struggled, I heard my pastor say something during one of the services that made me think deeply: "You cannot have the beauty and hope of Easter Sunday without the pain and ugliness of Good Friday."

I thought about that a lot and wondered about the pain I was going through. I finally concluded that I would not have peace and contentment if I did not allow myself to forgive this man. I soon realized that for me, the verse in Matthew meant not forgiving this man just once, but every time I felt the anguish overwhelm me. Sometimes, my anger was so deep I had to pray for him and myself— and forgive him several times a day. The first year after the incident I had struggled to even get out of bed, just wanting to curl up under the covers. But I had forced myself to get up and move one step at a time through the day. I had not wanted this man's actions to control my life, so I prayed myself through the day, leaning on God and His comfort.

Finally, on April 8, 2009, the anniversary date of the trauma came and went without me thinking about the incident. I only remembered it when my oldest daughter mentioned it two weeks later and commented about how well I was doing. I realized that I had no anxiety or trepidation as I had for the previous five years, each time that date approached.

Going through the process of forgiveness is different for everyone because everyone deals with pain differently. Yet certain common steps can help anyone facing unforgiveness. Though I am not a counselor or professional therapist, I offer these steps, developed from my own experience, only as a possible guide.

First, you have to face the offense. What happened? What is causing the anger? Were you able to tell the offender how much he/she hurt you? If it was a traumatic event, did you receive counseling? If you have buried the pain and hurt deep, you may have to let someone else help you peel back the layers to find the root of the pain you feel. This is tough, because our human tendency is to bury hurts.

You will probably have to relive every bit of hurt in order to truly face the offense, but with the help of a good counselor, you can come to a place where you can face the reason for your pain and anger and begin healing. Don't minimize what you went through—you have been hurt and it is critical that you acknowledge and face the pain. And don't try to do this alone.

Many times, I would find myself wailing and weeping before God, saying, "I hurt, Father. I hurt." It helped me to know that He knew and understood what I was going through. The tears helped me come to terms with grieving over the situation I was in. I felt like I had lost something when that man struck me. I took the time to regain my self-esteem and self-confidence.

Second, you need to make the courageous decision to forgive. This is where speaking to a counselor or trained medical professional can be of great value. I leaned on Scripture, too, and had many long conversations with my pastor and with God. This phase was the most difficult for me, as I had to come to terms with knowing that while the way I had been treated was unfair, there really wasn't anything I could do about it. I blamed myself for not going to the police or Human Resources right away, for wanting to protect the ministry so much that I had failed to protect myself. Through Scripture, though, I learned to have compassion for myself. Knowing that I had failed myself was hard for me, but once I came to terms with the situation, I found the courage to forgive my offender.

Third, once you have chosen to forgive an offense, you have to stick with it. It's not a one-time choice. Human nature makes us come back to reliving the hurts and offenses negatively so we can't let them go, but once you forgive someone, you have to try to forget the offense or learn to live with it constructively. This means not letting it take over your life; it means moving on in a positive way and learning to enjoy life again. It means not rehashing the offense with others (except a trained professional, pastor, or confidant who can help you move past it). This may take a year or more of concerted effort, especially in traumatic cases, to put it all behind you.

Fourth, surrendering and releasing the hurt, frustration, feelings of helplessness, and loneliness is the final step in forgiveness.

This is a difficult stage, especially if you are also dealing with depression. My ego and pride would not let me seek help right away. It was only when I found myself curled up in a ball crying and unable to care for my family that I knew I needed to seek help.

You deserve to be happy and fulfilled in your life. Believe that. Refuse to be a victim. Refuse to let an offender's action hold you hostage and stop you from being happy, from leading a fruitful and fulfilling life. Make the difficult choice to forgive and move on from the trauma that is holding you back.

Forgiveness is an issue that every race, nation, man, woman, and child is going to encounter at some time in their life. Learning how to forgive, and choosing to forgive, is one of the keys to living a more fulfilling life and creating a better world.

But, how do you find that deeper grace to forgive?

A few years ago, when I was speaking to a young man about forgiveness, he asked me, "How did you do it? How did you find that deep grace to forgive all that had been done to you?"

As I looked into my interviewer's eyes, I saw the deep pain reflected in them—a pain that made him ask the question that he had been searching an answer to for a very long time. A pain that I understood all too well.

And I knew that my answer had the potential to change this young man's life forever.

"It's simple," I said. "Your heart must desire it. Then, that desire to forgive must travel the eighteen inches or so between your heart and your head. That is the most difficult road to travel on the journey of forgiveness, because your mind must then make the decision to forgive. Once you make that courageous decision to forgive, the most important ingredient comes into play, and that is grace.

Grace can only be given by God. You have to ask God for the grace to forgive what you have done, or what was done to you."

Forgiveness is not easy, but it is possible with God's grace. It is a way of life—and a choice that one has to make for oneself. St. John Chrysystom said, "Nothing makes us so God-like as our willingness to forgive."

There are so many reasons given in the Bible about why we must forgive: because God first forgave us: because if we do not forgive others then God will not forgive us: because it is a mandate that the Bible gives us; but perhaps the best reason of all: because we grow more into the image of God when we are willing to forgive.

"Nothing makes us so God-like as our willingness to forgive."

15

Perhaps you have worked to forgive someone, but you are not sure if you have totally forgiven them. Maybe you still feel a little resentment or anger toward that person, or you think about what they did to you every time you see them. Or, you cross the street when you see them coming toward you.

Reverend Karyl Huntley said it best: "You know when you have forgiven someone when he or she has harmless passage through your mind."

Let me expand on this a little with an interesting situation I faced in June 2010. I was in St. Louis, Missouri, to be interviewed about my new book *The Courage to Forgive*, which had just been released. I walked into the huge convention center where the media was gathered to interview different authors. As I headed down the hallway, I saw the man who had hurt me deeply coming toward me. Imagine! I had not seen or spoken to this man in over seven years. This convention center was expecting thousands of people there that day, and the very first person I saw was this man. I couldn't believe my eyes! I knew that Satan was testing me. I had a major interview that morning to speak about my book and forgiveness, and Satan wanted to throw me off balance. But God had bigger plans. For a moment, I thought to myself, "Are you kidding me? Really?" And then, an incredible thing happened. This man continued to come toward me and I continued to walk toward him. He greeted me and I responded very cordially. He congratulated me on the release of my book, and I thanked him. We said goodbye. I felt no anger, no bitterness, and most of all, no fear. I had fully forgiven this man, and God had worked on my heart and filled me with the Holy Spirit. This man had no control over me. God had healed me completely.

—————⌇—————

"You know when you have forgiven someone when he or she has harmless passage through your mind."

—————⌇—————

I went on to give one of the best interviews of my life—so much so that the camera man came to me afterward and told me he would never forget the interview as long as he lived. It had changed his life. The same thing happened with three other people during interviews I gave that day. Lives were changed as the chains of unforgiveness were broken, one after the other.

That is how you know you have truly forgiven someone. They have no hold over you, and you feel no animosity toward them. You do not curse them, you do not wish ill for them, you do not intimidate them, and they do not intimidate you. You are able to pray for them and ask God to bless them.

Alexandra Asseily, the author of "The Garden of Forgiveness in Beirut" says, "Forgiveness allows us to let go of the pain in the memory, and if we let go of the pain in the memory, we can have the memory, but it does not control us. When memory controls us, we are then puppets of the past." I still remember every moment of that awful day I was brutalized and the days and weeks that followed, with great clarity—the sting of that man's hands striking my body, the shame of having to tell people what that man had done, and the fear I lived with for months because of the PTSD that was triggered by that event. I remember the injustice I felt for years. But, the pain no longer holds me captive.

There comes a time in everyone's life when you come to a fork in the road, where you have to make a decision that will forever impact your life. One path is the path of unforgiveness, which is strewn with bitterness, anger, unhappiness, sadness and most of all, a broken relationship with God. The other is the path of forgiveness, which leads to peace, happiness, contentment, a fulfilling relationship with God, and a life of blessings.

Perhaps Guy Finley said it best when he said, "There are those who will tell you why it is wise to never forget the pain of the past ... but if you look closely at the anger, sorrow, and bitterness that has hardened their faces, then you will also see why learning to forgive is the better of the two paths." Choose wisely which path you will take.

I don't know about you, but when I get to heaven, I want God to look at my face and see love, kindness, laughter, joy, compassion, forgiveness, and grace imprinted there. I want God to look at me and say, "Yes, another beautiful masterpiece." I certainly do not want Him to look at a face that has been hardened by anger, bitterness, sorrow, or marked by unforgiveness, and hear Him ask sadly, "Where is the masterpiece I created?"

If you truly want to experience God, to feel His presence, to be filled with the Holy Spirit, to feel the rush of Christ's love flowing through your very being in one incredible moment of grace after another, then you must find the courage to forgive. I have seen and experienced many valleys in my life, along with traumatic events that brought me to the brink of suicide, but I have known God's love through it all and I have enjoyed the view from the mountaintop as God stood by my side.

You too, can experience His great love. With faith and God's grace, you have the ability to turn the negatives in your life into positives. Today, you have the opportunity to change your life. You have the opportunity to make the courageous decision to forgive, to heal, and to find hope again.

If you are willing to do that I would encourage you to work through the following material, and write your answers on separate sheets of paper.

- I need to ask God to forgive me for _____
- I need to forgive myself for _____
- What family situation do I need to forgive?
- What can I do to reconcile with family members?
- Write an open letter to the person who has hurt you.

If you are ready to completely forgive yourself or the people who have hurt you, if you are willing to release yourself or them from any pain and anguish you have suffered, and you are prepared to pray that God would change your heart or bless the people who have hurt you, *then take these papers and destroy them*. Shred or burn them with all the hurt and anguish you have written on them. *Do not share* any of these papers with anyone, least of all the person who has hurt you. By destroying them, you will be releasing these situations to God.

At the end of the day, forgiveness is truly about trusting God. It's about being able to go through the hard times and seasons of trials, remembering that if God has allowed a difficulty to come into your life, He already knows how He is going to use that trial to bring you closer to Him and to shape you even more into the image of Christ. It is about trusting God in all things and being content in all things. It is about resting in the knowledge that He goes before you, walks beside you, and He has your back. All He asks is that you trust Him implicitly—in good times, and most especially, in bad times or times of deep trials.

Perhaps Mother Teresa of Calcutta said it best in the poem "The Final Analysis," her adaptation of the poem "Anyway" by Kent Keith. It says,

> People are often unreasonable, illogical, and self-centered;
> > ... Forgive them anyway!

> If you are kind, people may accuse you of selfish, ulterior motives;
> > ... Be kind anyway!

> If you are successful, you will win some friends and some true enemies;
> > ... Succeed anyway!

> If you are honest and frank, people may cheat you;
> > ... Be honest and frank anyway!

> What you spend years building, someone could destroy overnight;
> > ... Build anyway!

> If you find serenity and happiness, they may be jealous;
> > ... Be happy anyway!

> The good you do today, people will often forget tomorrow;
> > ... Do good anyway!

> Give the world the best you have, and it may never be enough;
> > ... Give the world the best you've got anyway!

> You see, in the final analysis, it is between you and God;
> It was never between you and them anyway.

FORGIVENESS PRAYER

Father God, thank You for today and for this opportunity to face the issues of un-forgiveness in my life. I love You, Father, and desire a deeper relationship with You and Your son, Jesus. I come to You with a humble and contrite heart, Father, and ask You to fill me with Your grace, mercy and compassion, as I choose freely today to forgive:

Myself (or another person's name): _____

for _____ (specific offense).

Father, I ask Your forgiveness for holding on to this offense, and I ask that You forgive me/this person and bless me/them with Your mercy and compassions, which are new every day.

And Father, I ask that if there are any other negative feelings in me, known or unknown, that You make them clear to me at this time, and that You purify me and cleanse me of these feelings. Please fill me with the Holy Spirit, and help me to regain the years that the locusts have stolen by my unforgiveness.

Father, as I embrace the plans that You have for me, I pray that You will not allow Satan to use the memories of these offenses to cause me to fall into unforgiveness again. Heal my heart and mind of these offenses, and most especially, heal the woundedness in my soul, so that I do not use that pain against those I encounter each day. Help me to break this cycle today.

Father, please bless me with courage and strength as I move forward in hope and healing. In the precious name of Jesus I pray. AMEN.